MA

AN ATTITUDE

MARRIAGE WITH AN ATTITUDE

How to Build an Exciting Marriage with a Fantastic Attitude!

BY

CHUCK & EILEEN RIFE

LOGOS TO RHEMA PUBLISHING
8210 E. 71ˢᵗ STREET #250
TULSA, OK 74133
1-918-488-9667

COPYRIGHT

MARRIAGE WITH AN ATTITUDE

COPYRIGHT© 1999/2000 by Chuck and Eileen Rife
LOGOS TO RHEMA PUBLISHING
FIRST PRINTING 1999

No part of this publication may be reproduced, stored in a retrieval system, or transmitted in any form, or by any means — electronic, mechanical, photocopying or otherwise without the prior written consent of the publisher or authors.

Written permission must be secured from the publisher or the authors to use or reproduce any part of this book, except for brief quotations in critical reviews or articles.

Scripture taken from the *NEW AMERICAN STANDARD BIBLE®*, © Copyright The Lockman Foundation 1960,1962,1963,1968,1971,1972,1973,1975, 1977. Used by permission.

Printed in the United States of America by Morris Printing in Kearney, NE.

ISBN: 0-7392-0504-8

Library of Congress Catalog Card Number: 00-90519

TABLE OF CONTENTS

DEDICATION:	VII
ACKNOWLEDGMENTS:	IX
FORWARD:	XI
ATTITUDE:	XIII
INTRODUCTION: ATTITUDE ACTS *"Building Your Attitude on the Acts of God"*	1
CHAPTER 1: ATTITUDE OF ADORATION *"Doting on Your Doll"*	11
CHAPTER 2: ATTITUDE OF CONFESSION *"Cuddling the Accused"*	49
CHAPTER 3: ATTITUDE OF THANKSGIVING *"Telling the Truth"*	71
CHAPTER 4: ATTITUDE OF SUPPLICATION *"Seeking the Source"*	97
EPILOGUE: ATTITUDE ACTS CONCLUSION	123
BIBLIOGRAPHY:	127
READING AND RESOURCE LIST:	129

DEDICATION

We dedicate this book to our parents, Lowell and Dorcas Rife and Robert and Lavina Hinkle, who have modeled a Christlike attitude throughout their married life.

ACKNOWLEDGMENTS

We thank our Heavenly Father for His unfailing wisdom and guidance throughout this entire project. To Him be all the glory!

A great big thank you to our three daughters, Rachel, Michelle and Stephanie. They prayed for us, washed dishes, cooked meals and ran errands, ad infinitum, while Mom and Dad discussed the manuscript and worked on the computer, typing, re-typing and re-typing!

A special thank you to Dave and Carolyn Peterson, Brett Roach, Dr. John DeVerter, Keith McCurdy, Sandy Albright, Martha Furman, Steve Price, Bob and Pat Gose, Joann Jones, Ann Mayhue, Jan Sherry, Joan McCann, Betty Bedwell, Doris Bradley, Rita Ward, David Mortellaro, Heather Farmer, Russ and Debby File, Dr. Gary Yates and Dr. Dan Mitchell for reviewing our manuscript and making valuable suggestions.

Thank you, Sue Reidel, for your encouraging and supportive attitude towards our manuscript idea and for making publication of our book a reality.

Diligent effort has been made to track down the source of each joke and quote included in these pages; if you find an error in the attributions, please notify the publisher or authors in writing so corrections can be made in future printings.

FORWARD

MARRIAGE WITH AN ATTITUDE

Chuck and Eileen Rife freshly, sometimes humorously, other times seriously, always personally, present marriage-improving attitudes that are good for all. As an improvement course, refresher course or starter course for marriage, the ageless truth is presented in contemporary reality that stimulates growth.

Few bring the insight and understanding that providing over 15,000 individual, marriage and family counseling sessions brings. Through a successful practice at Total Life Counseling, Inc. and Psychiatric Day Hospital, Chuck knows what attitudes need to be addressed. He also knows how to address them in a way that motivates improvement.

I have watched Chuck and Eileen interact over the years and admired their style. I have shared the platform and observed the warm response they generate. This couple walks the talk and walks it well.

Dave Peterson
President,
Total Life Counseling, Inc.
North American Director,
Medical Ministry International

ATTITUDE

Words can never adequately convey the incredible impact of our attitude toward life. The longer I live, the more convinced I become that life is 10 percent what happens to us and 90 percent how we respond to it.

I believe the single most significant decision I can make on a day-to-day basis is my choice of attitude. It is more important than my past, my education, my bankroll, my successes or failures, fame or pain, what other people think of me or say about me, my circumstances, or my position. Attitude keeps me going or cripples my progress. It alone fuels my fire or assaults my hope. When my attitudes are right, there's no barrier too high, no valley too deep, no dream too extreme, no challenge too great for me.

STRENGTHENING YOUR GRIP, by Charles R. Swindoll
c1982 Word, Inc. Nashville, TN
Used by permission of Insight for Living,
Anaheim, California 92806

INTRODUCTION
"ATTITUDE ACTS"

I remember asking Chuck a few years ago to write down the top two things he considered most important in encouraging him as a husband and as a man. Without hesitation, he responded with the twin A's — **ATTITUDE** and **APPRECIATION**. He desired me, as his wife to have an encouraging attitude, a teachable spirit, a willing response of support towards him, and he wanted me to build him up with appreciative words and actions. Needless to say, his aspirations for my attitude were lofty goals! I have failed many times in my clumsy attempts to fulfill his dream of a godly wife. Though difficult in my humanity to function as a Christian spouse, it is not impossible with the Almighty God of the Universe living within me to will and to do of His own good pleasure.

I really desire to love Eileen the way God wants me to, but I have failed more times than I care to think about. This became very apparent to me when I heard a message at Promise Keepers at RFK stadium in 1995. The message was that if the radiance was gone from my wife, which was there on our wedding day, the problem was not with her, but with me. I needed to take an inward look and see how I was contributing to the problems. I came home from that life-changing conference and examined how I needed to transform my life and attitudes. I determined, before God, to be the loving leader that my wife had been asking for all throughout our marriage, but I had not listened! Oh yes, I had heard the words many times, but I had never heard with **understanding**. I had never heard with **wisdom**, which **always leads to application**. I was now receiving the message with the "eyes to see" and the "ears to hear" that I was the responsible one. I was the one who needed to change. I was the one who needed to learn

Marriage With An Attitude

to lead. God impressed upon me that I was to be a leader to Eileen in the areas of humility, understanding, honor, love, intimacy, commitment, balanced ministry and in fruit manifestation — living before her a life that demonstrates the fruit of the Spirit of God — love, joy, peace, patience, kindness, goodness, faithfulness, gentleness and self-control (Galatians 5:22-23).

How many times have you heard a parent use one of these exclamations in confronting their child concerning an attitude problem? "Your attitude stinks! You've got a bad attitude. You need an attitude adjustment!" Maybe you have been there or you are that parent right now dealing with a disagreeable raunchy attitude. It's hard enough handling childish attitudes in your son or daughter, but imagine encountering the same attitude roadblocks in your spouse!

As I study God's marriage manual, the Bible, I encounter numerous and repeated exhortations in the area of attitude. One of my favorites is found in Philippians, chapter 2, where God clearly states the remedy for an attitude problem — **adopt the attitude or mind of Christ.**

Whoa! You think that sounds good in a Sunday morning sermon, but how does that relate to my everyday experience, where I live? You don't know my husband! You haven't lived with my wife! What has been acclaimed, as a "touch of heaven on earth" has been more of a "blast from hell" for you! **You wonder, "why isn't this working? What can I do to make this relationship better?"** You can be assured that you are on the right track when you begin asking these questions.

"If therefore there is any encouragement in Christ, if there is any consolation of love, if there is any fellowship of the Spirit, if any affection and compassion, make my

joy complete by being of the same mind, maintaining the same love, united in spirit, intent on one purpose. Do nothing from selfishness or empty conceit, but with humility of mind let each of you regard one another as more important than himself; do not merely look out for your own personal interests, but also for the interest of others. Have this attitude in yourselves which was also in Christ Jesus, who although He existed in the form of God, did not regard equality with God a thing to be grasped, but emptied Himself, taking the form of a bondservant, and being made in the likeness of men. And being found in appearance as a man, He humbled Himself by becoming obedient to the point of death, even death on a cross. Therefore also God highly exalted Him, and bestowed on Him the name which is above every name, that at the name of Jesus every knee should bow, of those who are in heaven, and on earth, and under the earth, and that every tongue should confess that Jesus Christ is Lord, to the glory of God the Father. So then, my beloved, just as you have always obeyed, not as in my presence only, but now much more in my absence, work out your salvation with fear and trembling; for it is God who is at work in you, both to will and to work for His good pleasure"(Philippians 2:1-13).

This passage, which Paul uses to instruct the Philippian Church, is also applicable to the Christian marriage, where true godly unity should begin. The exhortation to unity still applies, dear believer, even if you are living with a non-believer, because you may win him or her over by your humble attitude. In any case, Paul's directive is clear — **the mercy, love and compassion we have received from the Lord Jesus Christ should be exemplified through our lives to our mates**! True marital oneness can only be achieved with a mindset of humility.

Marriage With An Attitude

This does not mean we submit ourselves to every form of mental, emotional or physical abuse in the name of Christlike selflessness. We are not required to roll over and play dead, deny our feelings or pretend all is well when things are quite the contrary. True love and humility of mind requires responsible action on the part of the offending spouse. True love holds each other accountable and maintains healthy boundaries.

While many today are living in extremely abusive situations — and you may be one of those suffering right now in a similar way — **I fear the majority of professing Christians are destroying their marriages in much more subtle, but none the less, harmful ways.** Cutting words, harsh looks, the cold shoulder, the silent treatment are all games we each have played at one time or another.

Chuck and I are no exceptions in these areas. Numerous times one or both of us have been led down Satan's path of deception. What started out to be a perfectly innocent conversation about a trivial matter turned into a battle of the wills. I WILL be first. I WILL have the last word. I WILL not look foolish. I WILL have the upper hand. Satan finds great delight in chipping away at godly marriages over oftentimes, trivial things.

When our children were little, we used to enjoy special outings to an amusement-type restaurant that offered all sorts of games while you waited for your food to be delivered. One such pursuit the kids and we considered a delightful, yet frustrating, challenge, was the "Bop the Gopher on the Head" game. Maybe you have seen it. About ten gophers are hiding in their holes in a large machine ready to pop up any second (at the plop of a quarter or game token)! Our task was to take the attached bopper or mallet and bang the little guy on the head as soon as he popped up. The difficulty with this arrangement was that two or three would pop up almost simultaneously and in such scattered areas that we felt hopeless to catch them all. Of course the more we bopped, the more points we accumulated. I can still see the cunning grins on those gophers' faces, as if to say, "Ha, ha, catch me if you can, sucker!"

Our sin nature is about as deceptive as those tricky little gophers, popping up at unexpected times. We try in vain to bop it, but it keeps on rearing its ugly head time and time again. Satan laughs to himself when he dangles a juicy tidbit in front of us that lures our sin nature into action. Those juicy tidbits come in all kinds of forms. You may be lured into negative action by a phone call from your husband that he will be home late from work. You had plans. He must have forgotten. Doesn't he realize how important this is to me? As you converse within yourself, you get angrier and angrier, ready to explode when he finally does walk through the door.

True marital oneness can only be achieved when each partner sets his mind on humility. It is probably safe to say that most problems in marriage originate out of a selfish attitude. The spouse wants his/her own way, in essence, still walking around with that little undisciplined child inside. Each is focused so intently on his/her own needs, he/she cannot look beyond himself to the needs of the other, let alone the world. Marital oneness is not an end in itself, as delightful as it can be, but rather a means to accomplish the God-given task of reaching others for His Kingdom. The statement "they will know we are His disciples by our love" not only applies to the Church, but also to Christian mates. How are we to have strong churches if we do not have strong families first? The test of true Christianity begins at home where we tend to be more real with one another than anywhere else. We can find strength to build a good marriage if we set our minds on the Spirit, which is Life and Peace, rather than on the

Marriage With An Attitude

flesh which is death (Romans 8:6). Thus, a good working marriage requires a mindset (see also Romans 12:1-2; Colosians 3:2 & 12). How can we accomplish a godly mindset of humility?

First of all, it takes a decision — an act of the will. Set your mind is a directive, a command. Secondly, it takes a plan. Thirdly, it takes practice. Fourthly, it takes mega doses of prayer, individually and as a couple. If each spouse understands that the other is sincerely working on this area of humility, far less "speck pickin" will be going on. Each will be more focused on the log in his/her own eye. He/she will be more willing to forgive.

Furthermore, the fact that Christ gave Himself totally for your spouse and loves him/her completely gives you the ultimate cause to express Christlike love towards your mate, whether he/she is a believer or non-believer. William Hendriksen, well known for his New Testament commentaries, once wrote that "When grace changes the heart, submission out of fear changes to submission out of love, and true humility is born."

Therefore, the love of Christ in our hearts stirs us to action. When we ponder how much of His God-given rights and privileges Christ laid aside in order to redeem us for Himself, we are humbled. Our quests for humility must first, last and always take us to the foot of the Cross where Christ waits to provide His enabling power. When we consider what Christ gave up for us, it makes getting that last word in quite trivial and petty. Training the mind to review Christ's work of forgiveness in the midst of daily confrontations takes a concerted effort and continual practice. But the blessing of the cross reminder is always there for our review at any time. It may mean stopping in mid-sentence and saying to your spouse, "Let's pray" or "I'm so sorry; I forgot how much Christ has forgiven me, I forgive you, too." It may mean leaving the room until

Chuck & Eileen Rife

that stubborn, unyielding heart, can be wooed by the Holy Spirit, once again melted by God's grace and willing to surrender to the other in love. This is all a part of growing in grace and becoming true partners in the grace of life (1Peter 3:7). No easy task, but as we allow ourselves to be trained by godly discipline, we yield the peaceable fruit of righteousness (Hebrews 12:11).

Peace! What husband and what wife doesn't want peace to reign in their relationship by releasing the negative and reinforcing the positive? Peace comes when we know we've done right in the form of an, "I'm sorry; will you forgive me?" or in dropping a conversation that is out of control, refusing destructive words and threatening tones. Colossians 3:15 says, "And let the peace of Christ rule in your hearts."

We were called to be peacemakers. Peace is to be a way of life. Everyone desires peace. That's what keeps us coming back home at night, in hopes that perhaps we will discover that long awaited sanctuary we've dreamed about all our lives, a place of solace with Jesus and that special other that transcends earthly existence. I believe that's what God had in mind for husbands and wives when He designed the marriage union — a foretaste of heaven to come — a picture of His relationship with His beloved bride (Ephesians 5).

Personally, peace for me is a cozy fireplace, two overstuffed chairs or maybe a love seat, steaming cocoa and a snugly blanket wrapped around Chuck and me as we dream of the future TOGETHER! That's peace.

Godly humility also exemplifies the other fruits of the Spirit as well: love, joy, patience, kindness, goodness, faithfulness, gentleness, self-control (Galatians 5:22). The more we submit to the mind of Christ, the more power we have to enjoy the precious fruit of God's Spirit in our

Marriage With An Attitude

lives. If God Himself, in the form of Jesus, could lower Himself to take on the form of a man for our benefit, could we not quench that old pride for the benefit of our marriage relationships? Building our marriages on the acts of God means allowing ourselves to be silenced by who God is and what He has done for us and does do for us on a daily basis.

William Hendricksen sums up Jesus' ministry on earth so well in his New Testament commentary on Philippians. The following is our paraphrase of his excellent comments.

Jesus gave up his favorable relation to divine law. He had no burden of guilt in heaven. He chose to take this burden upon himself and carry it for us when he entered the world as a man (2 Corinthians 5:21). He relinquished his heavenly riches. Jesus, who owned everything because he made the world and all that is in it, became poor for us. He had no home or material possessions. He was constantly borrowing to meet His every earthly need. Furthermore, He gave up His glory in heaven. He felt this ever so intensely, especially in the garden the night He prayed before his crucifixion. From the depths of His agony He asked the Father to glorify Him in the Father's presence with the glory which He had with the Father before the world existed (John 17:4). And finally, He gave up His free and independent exercise of authority. He became a servant learning obedience by what He suffered, again for us! Please don't miss this — His love was so deep for us, He was willing to empty Himself with reference to His human nature. Keep in mind, He was still God, though now in human form. Surely, Christ's incarnation is the greatest mystery of power, wisdom and love ever known and always will be!

God's invitation to you, dear reader, is to imitate Christ in His humility. A godly attitude acts on behalf

of the other person. If you bear His name, then you belong to Him and you are no longer your own. You share in His life and have His life living within you. You are not alone. He is in you, with you and will never forsake you. **Rejoice in knowing fully that HIS POWER, HIS AUTHORITY, HIS GRACE and FORGIVENESS is yours every waking and every sleeping moment — even when you are not conscious of it!** You have the awesome privilege and responsibility of sharing in this extraordinary life with your mate — A LIFE CENTERED IN THE MIND OF CHRIST!

Perhaps you are not sure you belong to Christ in the first place. There has never been a time in your life when you personally called out to the Lord in faith believing that what He accomplished on the cross was for your forgiveness. We invite you to bow your head and heart right at this moment and tell God in your own words that you receive **His free gift of salvation through Jesus Christ.** We promise you on the authority of the Word of God that He will receive you as His own. You will embark on the most fascinating journey with your heavenly Father that you can ever imagine. The journey will not always be easy. In fact, at times it may seem more difficult than before you became a Christian, but we can tell you that **Jesus will never leave you nor forsake you and will walk with you always** as you walk in marriage, united in heart and set on one purpose — glorifying God in your union.

If you made the decision to receive Christ just now, write your name, date and decision in a place you can go back to often, perhaps a Bible, a journal or on the computer. Write and share with us what you have done. We'd love to hear from you and be of further encouragement.

Keep your eyes wide open before marriage, and half-shut afterwards!

Ben Franklin

1
ATTITUDE OF ADORATION
"Doting On Your Doll"

What do you value most? Have you ever, in one of your more reflective moments, thought about what your most prized possession is? Maybe yours is an old antique heirloom passed down through the family, or an expensive car that you polish every day and check meticulously for tiny, microscopic dents. Maybe your treasure is your house and you can't wait for another workweek to end so that you can spend the weekend fixing up your home. Perhaps your children are your prizes and you will stop at nothing to see that they have the finest clothing, education, and extra-curricular activities possible. Let's face it, if we are truly honest with ourselves, we have to admit that we are to some degree infatuated by the "stuff of life," the things we can see and our hands can handle. Our toys become the adoration of our lives. We often forget that the Almighty God of the universe is ultimately responsible for all that we possess. In the secret place of our idolatry we ignore the Heavenly Father who is to be honored and adored above all else.

Philippians chapter 2 quickly reminds me that a God who was willing to relinquish His heavenly throne for a season to identify with one like me, is a God who deserves my full and complete adoration. A God who is all-knowing, all-powerful, always present, utterly holy, just, and totally perfect in every way deserves my honor, respect, and praise! **Jesus Christ stands forever as the supreme role model for every Christian spouse.** He was the King of Kings and the Lord of Lords, yet He humbled Himself to the point of death in order to ransom

Marriage With An Attitude

us from the penalty of sin. We each are fashioned after God's image, not in the sense of being little gods, but to the degree that we each have the capacity to think, feel and act as God does.

When I look at my mate and realize that he is made in God's image I should be moved to prize him highly, to honor him, to consider him of great value. In a certain earthly sense he deserves a measure of adoration from me, not in the same way as I offer God my complete adoration, but certainly to some degree. I like Gary Smalley's analogy of the highly valued Stradivarius violin to that of my marriage partner. I wouldn't dream of throwing down my costly violin and stomping on it, but when it comes to my mate, I easily mistreat him, ridicule him and malign him either with my words or actions or both! Just as with the treasured Stradivarius, I should look at my mate, step back, take a deep breath and proclaim a hardy, "Wow! You are a highly prized treasure of my love. You deserve my praise, thoughtfulness, unselfishness, and my total love. I stand in awe of who God has made and is making you to be. You are an awesome creation of God!" If your spouse is a Christian the "wow" goes even further. Your mate is a Child of the King, a special divine workmanship, yes, and a work of art by the Master's hand and so are you if you have given your life to the King!

Viewing my mate as God views him helps my attitude take on a godly character. I will find it much easier to be of the same mind with him, not always fighting against his desires, but longing to hear him out, to support his dreams and to strive for loving compromises. I will find it easier to be united in spirit with him, intent on one purpose — namely to do God's will in our marriage — to be the partners God designed us to be, incorporating our individual personalities, interests and goals to expedite the common purpose of furthering His Kingdom.

Chuck & Eileen Rife

Wow, that all sounds so idealistic! Well, yes, it is. It is God's ideal for the Christian couple. How do we put these Biblical truths into shoe leather? How do we demonstrate in practical ways our desire to honor one another and take on a united front?

ADORATION THROUGH GOOD COMMUNICATION

One of the most practical ways to demonstrate honor and unselfishness in a marriage is through good communication. Effective communication is so vital in a marriage that it influences every other area in the relationship. Sometimes we feel frustrated with our mates because we think they do not understand where we are coming from and perhaps in reality they don't. After all, we each come from differing backgrounds, having learned our communication styles from our families of origin.

Some of us like to repress our thoughts and pretend we are not hurt or upset by the other person. Some of us enjoy avoiding issues altogether. We think that any confrontation whatsoever is not proper. Others of us may like to explode and push for our own way. We lose all reason and become demanding. We generally do drift to the styles we saw modeled before us in our early years.

Three primary styles come to mind when I consider marital communication.

➢ The Volcano or Exploder Style
➢ The Iceberg or Repressor Style
➢ The Biblical or Loving Compromise Style.

Marriage With An Attitude

I'm sure as you read through each of these examples you will find it easy to see which style is the most effective in achieving harmonious results.

VOLCANO STYLE — THE EXPLODER

John, coming in from work, throws down his briefcase and takes off his tie. "Oh, Hon, before I forget I've invited the boss and his wife over for Saturday lunch. We have some things to discuss on the Ellison project."

Mary immediately explodes. "What? You've got to be kidding! Amanda has her recital tomorrow and we are supposed to help with the refreshments. I told you about this three weeks ago. I can't believe you! Can't you remember anything? What's the matter with you?"

John steps back in shock. "Now wait just a minute. You knew I had this important project to get done and that I would need to spend extra time with the boss finishing it. What's wrong with me? How about you? Sounds like you have a problem with memory, too."

Mary has really had it by now. "Problem? The only problem I have is you! I can't believe I ever married you. All you ever think about is yourself! You're a thoughtless jerk! I've had it! You can fix Saturday lunch yourself! I won't be here!"

John, swept up in the escalating emotion of the moment, retorts, "Oh yeah? Well, you just do that; I don't need you anyway. All you ever do is complain, complain, nag, nag. Well, maybe I'm fed up, too. In fact, I've had it up to here. You can do what you want. The boss and his wife will be here tomorrow for lunch!"

Chuck & Eileen Rife

ICEBERG STYLE — THE REPRESSOR

Mark, coming in from work, takes off his jacket and briefly pecks his wife on the cheek. He grabs the paper and sits down to read, speaking as he goes. "Whew, I'm glad this week is over — Oh, Hon, I forgot to mention this, but I invited my boss and his wife over for Saturday lunch. We have some things to go over on the Ellison project. Hope you don't mind. I thought you and his wife might enjoy getting to know each other."

Allison thinks to herself as she straightens things. "Why does he always do this? I can't believe he's so thoughtless. Tomorrow is Saturday. What am I going to fix? The house is a mess! It's hopeless to try and talk to him about this — I've tried before! My words fall on his deaf ears. I guess I'll just go along. Oh, I'm so angry at him!"

Mark thinks to himself, "I'm sensing some resistance here, but I don't really care. I need these brownie points with the boss. She doesn't understand my work. She'll get over it." John speaks out loud to Allison, "So, how about it, Hon? Fix some of that wonderful chicken salad with croissants? Boy, I love that. I know they will, too."

Allison meekly gives in, "Oh, all right."

BIBLICAL STYLE — THE LOVING COMPROMISE

Harry, reading his paper, puts it down. He looks at his wife and speaks these words, "Hon, do you have a few minutes now to talk over something with me?"

Sue responds, "Sure. What do you have on your mind?" Sue puts her dishcloth down and comes to sit beside Harry.

Marriage With An Attitude

Harry explains his situation. "I have an important project I've been working on with the boss and we are getting closer to the deadline. He feels that we need to get together after work some evening or perhaps on a Saturday to finish up. I was wondering if I could invite him and his wife to lunch on Saturday to work on the project. How do you feel about that?"

Sue clears her throat. "Well, I understand you guys need to finish this up, but I don't know. Amanda and I had plans to go shopping for a new dress for her recital. I don't know how much time or energy I would really have to fix lunch and entertain."

Harry responds with a good idea. "What would you think about my ordering pizza or maybe Chinese and have it delivered to the house?"

Sue expresses concern. "Do you think we can really afford that right now?"

Harry reassures her, "Oh, I think we will be all right. I'll even help you straighten up the house. What do you think?"

Sue accepts the compromise. "Sounds like it could work. Amanda and I can do some cleaning tomorrow, also. Thanks for being willing to help."

A relieved Harry responds, "Sure thing."

As you can see from these brief examples, a given situation can take different turns depending on how a couple chooses to respond to the situation. The appropriate Biblical guidelines for resolving conflicts are outlined in Ephesians 4:25-32.

V.25
Therefore, laying aside falsehood, speak truth, each one of you, with his neighbor, for we are members of one another.

V.26,27
Be angry, and yet do not sin; do not let the sun go down on your anger, and do not give the devil an opportunity.

V.28
Let him who steals, steal no longer; but rather let him labor, performing with his own hands what is good, in order that he may have something to share with him who has need.

V.29
Let no unwholesome word proceed from your mouth, but only such a word as is good for edification according to the need of the moment, that it may give grace to those who hear.

V.30
And do not grieve the Holy Spirit of God, by whom you were sealed for the day of redemption.

V.31
Let all bitterness and wrath and anger and clamor and slander be put away from you, along with all malice.

V.32
And be kind to one another, tenderhearted, forgiving each other, just as God in Christ also has forgiven you."

The phrase, "laying aside falsehood," in verse twenty-five encourages honesty with one another in marriage.

Openness is absolutely essential in resolving conflict. Verse twenty-six urges you to control your anger. You

Marriage With An Attitude

may be prone to explode which may require a little time-out to cool off before you attempt discussion. **Avoid the use of words like always or never when addressing your mate.** Keep your voice at a reasonable pitch. Avoid name-calling.

Furthermore, verses twenty-six and twenty-seven deal with deciding on a good time to talk. Never argue in bed, in front of the kids, just before leaving for work or when there is not enough time to finish the disagreement. Never discuss a topic when you are hungry, angry, lonely or tired. Determine to resolve your differences before you retire at night or at least call a truce until you can decide on a good time to discuss the issue, preferably as soon as possible. In other words, close the day with a clean slate and a clear conscience before God and your spouse. Keep short accounts. Manage each day's problems as they occur. Don't allow issues to accumulate. Deal with one issue at a time and then forget it. Don't drag out the past. There are some things you will never agree on. Once you have dropped the matter, let it lie.

Be committed to a creative alternative (v.28). Find other ways of looking at an issue. Write down your best and worst case scenarios. Write down three or four creative compromises. Commit yourself to finding a Win/Win solution that works for both of you.

Be tactful in your presentation (v.29). Proverbs 15:1 says that "a gentle answer turns away wrath, but a harsh word stirs up anger." Be willing to admit when you are wrong and be quick to forgive. Identify any pride, worry, jealousy, hatred, anger, spite, frustration, laziness, fear, exhaustion, etc. that may be triggering a problem. Don't try to put most of the blame on your mate.

Before you begin discussion, make sure you are arguing about the right thing. If the boss just chewed you out, don't take it out on your wife's cooking. If you're physically exhausted yourself, don't blame her for being frigid.

Keep your discussion private (v. 30). Avoid public humiliation. Even if you win the battle you will surely lose the war. People who go public do so to get pity. Keep the conflict between the two of you and by all means let the Holy Spirit of God help.

Finally, restore your friendship (verses 31 and 32). Put off your anger with all of its trappings and put on godliness exhibiting kindness, tender hearts and forgiveness.

According to John Powell in his book, *Why Am I Afraid to Tell You Who I Am?*, we tend to communicate on five different levels, **five being the least intimate and one being the most intimate.** The more we can learn to incorporate all five with our mates, the better our communication skills will become, thus enhancing our relationships.

LEVEL FIVE — CLICHES

When employing Level 5 communication, you are simply conversing with your spouse as you would with a casual acquaintance. You might exchange shallow cordialities such as, "How are you?" and "I'm fine."

LEVEL FOUR — REPORTING THE FACTS

Level 4 communication steps into a new arena of conversation, employing facts learned. For instance, you might say, "Did you hear about Grace and Howard? She's pregnant again."

Marriage With An Attitude
LEVEL THREE — IDEAS AND JUDGMENTS

You feel comfortable enough in the relationship by now to offer some personal ideas and opinions. "Woman's place is in the home," you might say or "Why shouldn't I take a part time job? We need the money."

LEVEL TWO — FEELINGS AND EMOTIONS

This is where many men have trouble crossing the line. Women have an easier time expressing emotion, and often are frustrated with their seemingly stubborn or unfeeling husbands. Some women insist on communicating at this level at all times, which simply does not work, either. She might say, "How do we handle these payments? If the bills get any bigger — I'll go crazy!" or "I just can't take another long trip with the kids in that car. We've got to get something bigger or I'll go nuts."

LEVEL ONE — TRUTHFUL COMMUNICATION

Now you feel comfortable enough with your spouse to be totally honest about your feelings, your thoughts, plans and dreams. You are willing to work through to a solution. You might say, "I don't know if I really want that new job. I'm not sure I've got what it takes to be a manager."

I like the anonymous e-mail we received over the computer a few months back. The person who wrote it sure had a handle on this problem of communication, particularly between the sexes. Because of the differences between males and females, we often find it hard to relate to each other. Here is one female's perception of a male's thoughts and the intent behind them:

Chuck & Eileen Rife

WHAT A GUY REALLY MEANS:

- It's a guy thing. Really means... There is no rational thought pattern connected with it, and you have no chance at all of making it logical.

- Can I help with dinner? Really means... Why isn't it already on the table?

- Uh huh. Sure, honey, or Yes, dear. Really means... Absolutely nothing. It's a conditioned response.

- It would take too long to explain. Really means... I have no idea how it works.

- I'm getting more exercise lately. Really means... The batteries in the remote are dead.

- We're going to be late. Really means... Now I have a legitimate excuse to drive like a maniac.

- Take a break, honey, you're working too hard. Really means... I can't hear the game over the vacuum cleaner.

- That's interesting, dear. Really means... Are you still talking?

- Honey, we don't need material things to prove our love. Really means... I forgot our anniversary again.

- You expect too much of me. Really means... You want me to stay awake.

- That's women's work. Really means... It's difficult, dirty, and thankless.

Marriage With An Attitude

- You know how bad my memory is. Really means…I remember the theme song to F Troop, the address of the first girl I ever kissed and the Vehicle Identification Numbers of every car I've ever owned, but I forgot your birthday.

- Oh, don't fuss. I just cut myself, it's no big deal. Really means…I have severed a limb, but will bleed to death before I admit I'm hurt.

- I do help around the house. Really means…I once put a dirty towel in the laundry basket.

- Hey, I've got my reasons for what I'm doing. Really means…I sure hope I think of some reasons pretty soon.

- I can't find it. Really means…It didn't fall into my outstretched hands, so I'm completely clueless.

- What did I do this time? Really means…What did you catch me doing?

- I heard you. Really means…I haven't the foggiest clue what you just said, and am hoping desperately that I can fake it well enough so that you don't spend the next three days yelling at me.

- You look terrific. Really means…Oh, good grief, please don't try on one more outfit. I'm starving.

- I missed you. Really means… I can't find my socks, the kids are hungry and we're out of toilet paper.

- I'm not lost. I know exactly where we are. Really means…I'm lost. I have no idea where we are, and no one will ever see us alive again.

Chuck & Eileen Rife

- We share the housework. Really means...I make the messes, you clean them up.

- This relationship is getting too serious. Really means...You're cutting into the time I spend with my truck.

- I don't need to read the instructions. Really means... I am perfectly capable of screwing it up without printed help.

Sounds like I came down pretty hard on the male of our species, but since I am the one writing this section, I took some liberties. Let's face it, girls, we females have our own brand of slippery communication. One of the all time favorites is, "But you are suppose to know what I want before I tell you. If I have to tell you, it takes all the fun and mystique out of it." Uh, isn't that the point of good communication? We do not live in a fairy tale world as many of us romantics grew up believing. In reality, our shining knights on sturdy white steeds are a bit tarnished in the armor department and fail to meet our every expectation for the perfect union in the happily ever after.

Chuck admits that he failed Mind Reading 101 in college. Our expectations in communication can be unrealistic at times, gals, as evidenced by one person's version of the female rules.

THE RULES

1. The female ALWAYS makes the rules.

2. The rules are subject to change at any time WITHOUT PRIOR NOTIFICATION.

3. No male can possibly know ALL the rules.

Marriage With An Attitude

4. If the female suspects the male knows all the rules, she must IMMEDIATELY CHANGE SOME OR ALL of the rules.

5. The female is NEVER wrong!

6. If it seems the female is wrong, it is because of a flagrant misunderstanding, which is the direct result of SOMETHING THE MALE DID or SAID WRONG.

7. If rule number 6 applies, then the MALE MUST APOLOGIZE immediately for causing the misunderstanding.

8. The female can change her mind at ANY TIME.

9. The male must never change his mind without THE EXPRESS WRITTEN CONSENT FROM THE FEMALE.

10. The female has the right to be upset or angry AT ANY TIME.

11. The male must remain calm at all times, unless the female WANTS him to be angry or upset.

12. The female must UNDER NO CIRCUMSTANCES ALLOW THE MALE TO KNOW whether or not she wants him to be angry or upset.

Note: Males that abide by these rules will have a very successful and happy relationship with the female!
—Anonymous—

Chuck & Eileen Rife

To achieve a union of understanding, we must lay our cards on the table and learn to say what we mean and ask for what we want. We must understand that we each come to a conversation with differing personality styles, thoughts and goals. Honoring one another means appreciating the differences between us.

In his video series, *Hidden Keys to Loving Relationships*, Gary Smalley expresses personality styles in the form of four different animals. By isolating your individual style and that of your mate, you can actually reduce conflict, because you have a greater understanding of why the other person reacts or responds the way he or she does.

The **LION** personality is a born leader, a very dominant person who takes charge and makes things happen. They can be overbearing at times, pushy, and intimidating to people. They like to act quickly and may not be prone to long discussions. They may exhibit an exploder style of communication. They will need to relax and learn to express their anger in appropriate ways.

The **OTTER** personality is the party animal, always looking for a good time. They are fun loving, entertaining, and enthusiastic motivators. They are full of creative ideas, but do not always follow-through on them. They tend to have numerous friendships, all of which are rather shallow. They are optimistic, rather impulsive and spontaneous. Realizing this in your mate will help you see why they communicate the way they do.

The **GOLDER RETRIEVER** is the most sensitive of all the personality types. They shun confrontation so they may communicate using the repressor style. They enjoy structure and are highly loyal. They are nurturing and warm. They can be easily wounded and will hold on to a grudge relentlessly.

Marriage With An Attitude

The **BEAVER** type is a perfectionist. They enjoy accuracy. Because they value order to such a high degree, they can make others feel uncomfortable. They are serious, insist that they finish what they start and demand that all things be done right.

When Chuck and I first learned about the personality types described as different animals, we had fun determining our individual styles. Actually, the exercise was quite enlightening, as we came to realize why we responded to each other the way we did sometimes. You see, Chuck is primarily a Golden Retriever, with some beaver and lion tossed in. I am primarily a lion, with some otter and beaver mixed in.

Early on in our marriage, my Golden Retriever husband would avoid conflict and confrontation and would go into silent mode when challenged. Frustrated by what I perceived was a lack of concern or sensitivity to my needs, I (as the Lion that I am) pushed him and verbally egged him on until finally he would get mad. In my mind, anger was a better response than no response at all.

After years of this pattern, we finally came across Gary Smalley's material. The category styles made sense to us. Thereafter, when we operated out of our personality types we tended to chuckle over the differences rather than become angry or frustrated. Over the years, we have attempted to adopt other styles into our personalities when our primary modes exhibited pronounced weaknesses.

For example, Chuck's natural tendency as a Retriever is to shun confrontation. Realizing this he endeavors to incorporate some lion traits when handling difficulties. He is more apt to say what he thinks or wants and come to a resolution. Combining his natural Retriever tendencies, which encourage warmth and nurturing, with some Lion traits that encourage verbal openness, aids in more effective communication between us.

I, on the other hand, am normally quick to confront, often before I have thought through an issue thoroughly. Aware of this tendency, I try to be less overbearing and impulsive and more thoughtful before presenting my viewpoint. In this way, I am blending Lion and Retriever qualities to enhance better communication and to also identify with Chuck's Retriever mode.

Simply identifying your own unique style and that of your spouse can help you learn to use your strengths and blend your differences to love one another. Learning to adjust to the other person and bring yourself into balance can go a long way in achieving marital harmony. You must decide to be softer if you are a Lion. You must make a point of following through on your plans if you are an OTTER. You need to practice confrontation if you are a Golden Retriever. And if you are a Beaver, you need to relax and take life a little less seriously.

Chuck often deals with clients who are having difficulty honoring their spouses because of poor communication skills. Several things are helpful when communication is blocked.

PRACTICAL HELP FOR EFFECTIVE COMMUNICATION

1. WRITE: Each person writes on paper his or her view of what is being discussed.

2. READ: Each person reads what the other person has written. Each person looks for areas of agreement. Notice multiple topics (you can only resolve one issue at a time).

Marriage With An Attitude

3. REPORT: Each person reports verbally what he or she has read.

4. QUESTION: Each person asks the other if they have reported their view accurately.

5. DISCUSS: Build on the areas of agreement. Explore the alternatives — Brainstorm. Choose the best alternative (no alternative will be perfect). Increase your "understanding" of each other and then you will both win. Use "speaker cards" as needed to avoid interrupting. The speaker card can be any card with the word speaker written on it. It is used to take turns in the conversation. Remember the ultimate goal is to love, honor and prefer one another.

6. REPEAT: If communication breaks down begin writing again. This will seem strange and stilted to some, but it will work, if you do it! You will be surprised how quickly you will outgrow this technique. This technique is helpful whenever difficult decisions must be made.

7. REJOICE: You can now confront difficult problems together successfully. You can now share with other couples what you have learned.

EPHESIANS 4:25-32

Thinking before we speak to our mates is a matter of Holy Spirit discipline. An example of a poor statement would be, "You make me so mad!" At Total Life Counseling, we encourage people to say, "I *feel* very angry and hurt, **when you** ignore me when I'm talking to you, **because** it seems like you don't care about me or what I am saying. I **would prefer** that you either pay attention to me or tell me when we could talk."

Writing down this process can be helpful as you train yourself to think before you speak.

I FEEL:
_____
How do you feel about the other's behavior or actions?

WHEN YOU:
_____
What exactly did they do?

BECAUSE:
_____
Explain how the behavior or actions affect you.

I WOULD PREFER:
_____
What behavior would be acceptable to both of you?

WHAT DO YOU THINK? *LISTEN* to them *NOW*.

Keep in mind that you, as a couple are not the enemy. Oftentimes, we turn our issues into grounds for attacking the other person, when the mate is not the problem, the topic is! Keep the topic before you and focus on the process of resolution. Work together as a team to come to an agreement based on your writings. Satan delights in warring against our souls. Nothing makes him happier than seeing Christian couples tear each other apart sometimes over minor issues.

Communication is threefold. It involves effective listening, effective talking and effective understanding. Trying to understand another person's opinion or point of view does not automatically mean that you agree with or

Marriage With An Attitude

endorse that opinion. Allow for differences of opinion and remember that the effort to understand what each other is conveying actually represents enriched communication. In other words, we can disagree without quarreling. Our listening to understand demonstrates our character and reveals our desire to honor the other person.

As you seek to honor one another through your communication, be available to the other person, accept responsibility for your own thoughts, acts, values, feelings and perceptions you contribute to the conflict. Be flexible and willing to make some degree of change, so that you both can move toward a joint solution. Be specific as you focus on a practical outcome that is within the range of possibility. And finally, be clear in your presentation of your point(s). Your words, tone of voice, facial expression, posture, must all be congruent with each other and with the setting in which they are said.

ADORATION THROUGH COMMITMENT

Remember the love that drew you together. Thank God for this and refresh yourselves in commitment to each other and to God in the vows you made to one another on your wedding day.

Employ Ed Wheat's "B E S T" prescription as described in his book, *Love Life*.

B E S T

B — Blessing: Doing or saying kind things. Praying for one another. When married couples pray together the divorce rate drops to less than 3 percent.

E — Edify: "Build up; strengthen" by complimenting often. Go out on dates, write each other notes and leave

Chuck & Eileen Rife

them around the house. Pour on the praise and appreciation.

S — Sharing: Share verbally your ideas, goals and emotions, letting each other know how you feel and think. This often requires work and patience. Share good times again, have fun, remember and do the things you did when you were dating. Join the Society of Childlike Persons and have fun together.

T — Touching: Nonsexual touching builds emotional love and intimacy. Men often think touch must always be sexual, but women crave EMOTIONAL INTIMACY. This builds Trust and is a wonderful investment in your marriage.

Take a minute right now. Step back from your spouse and shout an enthusiastic "Wow! You are awesome! I love you with all my heart. I honor you in the Lord." After he picks himself up off the floor, you can hug and rejoice together in your mutual admiration.

One of the grandest displays of honor I have ever observed in a marriage was Dad Rife's care of Mom during her five-year battle with Alzheimer's disease and breast cancer. Dad was relentlessly committed to helping Mom fight her illness. He prepared special foods for her daily, gave her prescribed injections and medications, kept track of medical appointments and new breakthroughs in scientific technology, all the while keeping the family informed of her progress.

When Mom was living out her final days, bedridden at home and under the care of Hospice, Dad was right there by her side. Even when she slipped away from us into a coma, Dad persisted in caring for her at home for her final two weeks on this earth.

Marriage With An Attitude

I remember Mom's last day with us. Chuck and I had driven up to Ohio for the weekend to see how the folks were doing. We did not realize until we arrived just how close the end was. Cathy, my sister-in-law and I were in the room with Dad and Mom. Other family members were milling about the house. The five youngest grandchildren had just come into Grandma's room to sing her a couple of her favorite songs. Mom loved music and I believe to this day that she heard the sweet songs of her grandchildren, that somehow the quiet flow of the music relaxed her and gave her permission to leave her earthly dwelling and move on to even greater angelic sounds in heaven.

As Dad knelt by Mom's bedside and lovingly held her hand, he gently spoke with her, assuring her that it was all right to go. I remember Dad saying over and over again, "It's Okay to go, Honey. Let Jesus take you." Not long after as Dad was kneeling by her and bowing his head (perhaps in prayer, I don't know), Mom's eyes shot open and she lunged forward in the bed. Her eyes closed and she was finally at complete rest.

Watching on, Cathy and I burst into tears and held one another as Dad came over to console us with his hugs. He was at peace now too and confident of God's will.

Mom died two weeks before her fiftieth wedding anniversary. Right up to the end, I witnessed the loving care and faithfulness of a man who cherished and adored his wife, for better or for worse. What a treasured legacy for his family to observe! I can only say through grateful tears, "Thank you, Dad. Thank you for your example of a godly committed spouse."

Chuck & Eileen Rife

ADORATION THROUGH GODLY LEADERSHIP

I am impressed as a man and head of my home that another way I need to show honor towards Eileen is in the area of leadership. God has called me to be the leader of my home, whether or not I always relish the role. I believe this God-given leadership takes on several forms.

1. HUSBANDS ARE TO BE LEADERS IN HUMILITY.

When my family and I went on a two-week mission's trip to India, one of the requests made by the Indian pastors in Madras was that I conduct a counseling seminar as part of the three day pastor's conference. The Indian pastors were eager to learn how to apply the Scriptures practically to their everyday concerns, particularly in the area of marriage and the family.

As pastors stood around me in a circle in our hot, stifling meeting room, I opened the Bible to John 13:5. I read, "After that he (Jesus) poured water into a basin and began to wash the disciples' feet, and to wipe them with the towel wherewith he was girded." I explained to these dear men that in order to truly love our wives as Christ loves the Church, we must first of all humble ourselves before them. I suggested that they might literally try sitting on the floor before their wives and express honor to them. At this point, I heard giggles and chuckles from some of the men.

One man who had decent command of the English language explained to me that the reason the men were laughing was because they would not dream of sitting on the floor in front of their wives. You see, in Indian culture, the wife is a second-class citizen. She is not considered an equal. The advent of Christianity into the culture has elevated the status of women to some degree, but not to the extent that it should be.

Maybe some of you men are similar to the Indian pastors who found it difficult to humble themselves, even physically before their wives. American culture elevates the status of women, but your pride hinders you from modeling humility before her. You fear that she will think less of you as a man if you practice humility, when in fact, the opposite is actually true. When your wife sees you admitting your faults, asking forgiveness, or shedding tears in front of her, you loom bigger and bigger in her eyes. The way to respect is the way of humility. He who desires to be first, should go last.

2. MEN ARE TO BE LEADERS IN UNDERSTANDING AND HONOR.

If we expect our wives to understand and honor us, then we need to do the same for them. First Peter 3:7-8 urges husbands to live with their wives in an understanding way, giving her honor, since she is the weaker vessel. Whether this refers to physical, emotional, or spiritual weakness, the point is Scripture specifies that she is the weaker vessel and should be treated gently, with kindness and tenderness. Behavior such as this will encourage effective answer to prayer as you serve Him together as equals, but with differing functions in the relationship.

I came across a story told by Phil Myers in his writing, *Family Seminar Syllabus* that illustrates beautifully the need for men to honor their wives.

Chuck & Eileen Rife

JOHNNY'S SEVEN COW WIFE

Johnny was an African chief. Now the custom in Johnny's part of Africa was that young men would buy their wives for a dowry of one cow, but Johnny had paid seven cows.

Once in a while you would hear of a man who had a two-cow wife. He might have paid two cows because she was extremely talented, or wise or beautiful. Perhaps her father was a chief or a witch doctor or someone well thought of. But no one had a seven-cow wife. Only in the legends and tribal stories did you ever hear of a seven-cow wife. But Johnny had one.

An American missionary went to see this chief one-day to ask him what it was that made his wife so special, so rare. As they sat and talked in Johnny's home, Johnny's wife came to serve tea and crumpets, or whatever African wives serve their company and the missionary got to meet this truly rare woman.

Finally the missionary asked his host what made this woman so special. How did he know before he married her that she was worth seven cows? What made him pay the price?

Then Johnny said, "When I was a young man I made a decision that someday I would have a seven-cow wife. No matter what anyone else did, I would settle for nothing less. I worked hard to earn the dowry, but as I began to look for such a woman I couldn't find her. There were no girls who were worth what I had determined to have, but I would not settle for less. So I found a girl, just an ordinary girl and I PAID THE PRICE. I paid the price and she became a SEVEN-COW wife."

Marriage With An Attitude

Dear husband, are you willing to pay the price to have your wife become that kind of a woman? Are you willing to sacrifice out of love so that God is free to turn your wife into the woman He wants her to be? The cost is high but the result is great!

3. HUSBANDS ARE TO BE LEADERS IN LOVE AND INTIMACY.

When I do not see the radiance in Eileen that I saw on our wedding day, I need to ask myself what I may have done or not done to contribute to her difficulty. I am to love Eileen as I love my own body (Ephesians 5:28-29). I need to seek meaningful ways to reach out to her. What may minister to Eileen may be different from what ministers to your wife. You need to be a student of your wife, learning what woos her heart to you.

Dr. Gary Chapman, a North Carolina pastor and counselor, has determined that there are actually five languages of love: words, gifts, touch, acts of service and quality time. My favorites are words and touch.

If your wife responds to words of praise and affirmation, she will enjoy hearing you say things like, "Thank you." You really did an outstanding job on dinner" or "Oh, Hon, I really love your new dress."

If she likes gifts she may be giving to you constantly and does not understand why you never bring her anything. We tend to subconsciously do for another what we want done for ourselves. You need to surprise her with a gift every now and again to light her fire.

Your wife may constantly nag that you don't spend enough time with her. When you are home, she may perpetually be at your side. This is probably because she is a person who highly values quality time. Spend it with her. Your investment will pay off.

If your wife is always craving hugs and lots of touching, she finds her fulfillment in your relationship primarily through that avenue. Indulge her. You will enjoy it too. But don't always insist that every touch lead to sex. She probably is not looking for consummation every time.

Finally, your wife may yearn for acts of service. Do little things around the house without her asking. She will love you for it and you will come to appreciate her role as homemaker a little bit better.

Taking the time to discover your wife's primary and secondary love language will reap tremendous dividends in your marriage. As you reach out to meet her specific needs, she will surely reciprocate, as women are responders by nature. Eileen enjoys acts of service primarily and quality time secondarily. I try to remember to include some form of these in my daily routine.

4. HUSBANDS NEED TO BE LEADERS IN COMMITMENT.

As soon as we say "I do" fellows, we are committed for life. We have made the choice to leave father and mother and cleave to our wives. Some people seem to have trouble really leaving their parents. Even after marriage, the financial and emotional umbilical cord is still intact. Make sure you have severed those ties and can stand on your own two feet. Honor your parents, ask for advice, but by all means be the head of your home and the final authority in all decisions. Don't give in to the temptation to throw in the towel on your marriage over every struggle that emerges. Stand strong. No matter what others do, declare YOUR MARRIAGE a LIFELONG COMMITMENT!

5. MEN ARE TO BE LEADERS IN BALANCED MINISTRY

This area could be an entire book in itself. So many people today are over committed, not to their marriages, but to everything under the sun. They are committed to an abundance of church work, volunteer work, job, recreational pursuits and the list goes on. One tiny, but difficult word I employ is, "NO." Yes, learn to say, "NO." That small two-letter word will free your life beyond imagination. Before you can say, "No" you must sit down and determine your priorities in life. As I have wrestled with this issue, I believe my primary concerns in life should fall in this order:

1. My fellowship with God.

2. My fellowship with my wife and then children (in that order).

3. My work-related responsibilities.

4. My church-related responsibilities.

Sometimes, these areas are not as black and white as they appear on paper. Sometimes, the areas overlap. At any given moment, I may be required to determine my priority for that particular time and situation. **BALANCE is definitely the key word when considering priorities**. If I am spending all my time at church, attending one meeting after another or constantly out on visitation and I have not spent adequate time with my family, then something is amiss. On the other hand, if I am missing Sunday services a majority of the time to be out on the lake with my wife and kids I am once again out of balance. The point I am making is I need to determine my priorities and be a model for Eileen in the area of a BALANCED LIFESTYLE.

6. HUSBANDS NEED TO BE LEADERS IN FRUIT MANIFESTATION.

Finally, our wives need to see us practicing real Christianity, not just talking about it. We need to be patient, kind, controlled, loving, joyful and peaceful, even as Christ was while on this earth. A tall order, I realize, but as in all matters of the faith walk, we are ever so dependent on the Holy Spirit's infusion of power and grace!

Being examples in these areas of leadership can show our wives that we truly value them, enough to allow God to change us into the men of God He desires us to be for His service in our homes, communities and churches.

As we close this chapter on honoring your spouse, specifically in the areas of communication, commitment and leadership take some time to flip through the next few pages of Practical Helps. Do the exercises individually and as a couple. Put the tips into practice as you go about your daily routine and in so doing bring honor both to your spouse and to the God who loves you and values you highly! Spend some time each day doting on your doll! He or She will adore you for it!

PRACTICAL HELPS

Marriage With An Attitude
HOW TO HONOR GOD

The most important step in life is receiving Jesus Christ as your personal Saviour and thus establishing a relationship with God. Your time with God on a daily basis can make or break your marriage.

CONSIDER THE FOLLOWING QUESTIONS AND ANSWER THEM AS HONESTLY AS YOU CAN:

1. Do I currently have a time each day when I get alone with God in His Word and prayer?

2. Do I have a specially appointed place to meet with God?

   Mine is my prayer chair early in the morning before anyone else gets up. Somehow I feel closer to God in the stillness. Yours may be at the kitchen table in the afternoons before the kids get home from school or at night in your bedroom before you retire. The point is to establish a regular time and place to meet with God every day. Just as you eat regular meals, feed on God's Word daily.

3. As a man, do I lead my family in devotions or do I leave that area of our family life to my wife?

Chuck & Eileen Rife

We find taking a fifteen-minute devotional time or date with Jesus right after breakfast most effective for our family.

4. Is there anything in my life I need to put away in order to put God first in my life? TV time, over-commitments on the job, at church or with friends. Remember that even good things taken to extreme can rob you of fellowship time with God if you are not careful. **Balance is the key word here.**

HOW TO HONOR YOUR MATE

RATE YOUR MARRIAGE FROM ONE to TEN. ONE IS LOW AND TEN IS HIGH

Where would you rate your marriage today?

Where would you like your marriage to be?

What one thing could move it closer to where you want it?

WHEN YOU ARE IN CONVERSATION WITH YOUR MATE ABOUT A TOPIC...

Do you tend to run, avoid the issue or repress your true feelings?

Do you tend to fight, considering this a bout to determine your worth and significance?

Do you tend to cloud the issue with multiple topics? Do you seek a solution-focused answer with no goal of personal winning?

Marriage With An Attitude

WHEN YOU TALK...

Do you tend to use only clichés with your spouse?

Do you simply report the facts?

Do you offer your ideas and judgments on an issue?

Do you share your feelings and emotions?

Do you strive for open, truthful communication?

MEN ON A SCALE OF ONE TO TEN, RATE YOURSELF IN EACH AREA OF LEADERSHIP:

_____Humility

_____Understanding and Honor

_____Love and Intimacy

_____Commitment

_____Balanced ministry

_____Fruit manifestation

If you gave yourself a five or lower in any area, what are you doing now to merit this number?

_____
_____
_____
_____

Build on your number to increase your score. With a desire to do better and with God's enablement, YOU CAN!

In the area of love and intimacy try to determine your wife's top two love languages. Ask her if you are right. She can then try to guess your top two. This can become a fun game.

HOW TO COMMUNICATE PROPERLY

SET ASIDE A SPECIFIC TIME TO PRACTICE THE FOLLOWING EXERCISE

A. **WRITE**: Each person writes on paper his/her view of what is being discussed.

B. **READ:** Each person reads what the other person has written. Each looks for areas of agreement. Notice multiple topics (you can only resolve one issue at a time).

C. **REPORT:** Each person reports verbally what he/she has read.

D. **QUESTION:** Each person asks the other if he/she reported his or her view accurately.

E. **DISCUSS:** Build on areas of agreement. Explore the alternatives/brainstorm. Choose the best alternative (no alternative will be perfect). Increase your

Marriage With An Attitude

understanding of each other and you will both win. Use speaker cards as needed to avoid interrupting. Remember the ultimate goal is to love, honor and prefer one another.

F. **REPEAT:** If communication breaks down, begin writing again. This will seem strange and stilted to some, but it will work, if you do it! You will be surprised how quickly you will outgrow this technique. This technique is helpful whenever difficult decisions must be made.

G. **REJOICE:** You can now confront difficult problems together successfully. You can now share with other couples what you have learned. You are doing Ephesians 4:25-32. Knowing Scripture is great, but applying it to our lives is where the Holy Spirit's power comes alive.

*Marriage is called a three-ring circus:
The engagement ring,
the wedding ring,
and
the suffeRING!*

Rachel A. Park

2
ATTITUDE OF CONFESSION
"Cuddling the Accused"
♥

The other evening I was driving (another word for that is flying) to pick up Chuck after work. I knew I was going to be late and was mentally rehearsing all my good excuses to have ready when I opened his office door. Thankfully, I landed the car squarely between the parking space lines, screeched to a halt and fumbled to open the car door. Clutching my purse, I zipped from the car to Chuck's office as if in flight again. Clearly my feet were not on the ground yet, let alone my head. I was still in a frenzy of thought when I pulled open the heavy office door. Guess who had been waiting for me for an hour? I was ready! My guns were loaded and both barrels were aimed at my unsuspecting victim.

Picking up his lunch container and briefcase, my dear husband commented, "Where have you been? I thought you were lying out on the highway somewhere."

My guns accidentally went off. I did not want them to, but they did anyway, as if having a mind of their own. I immediately blurted out. "Lying out on the highway! Such leisure is not possible on this tight, frantic schedule. How can you possibly think I would take time to LIE out on the highway? I've done nothing but rush to get here."

Somehow, I think I missed his point. In my desperate attempt to defend myself from assault, I charged in like the light brigade, not able to detect the concern in Chuck's voice.

Marriage With An Attitude

After firing off a few more choice rounds on the way home we both retreated to our sides of the car and played wounded soldiers for the rest of the evening.

As is often the case, I awoke the next morning with the startling realization that my dear, sweet, husband *really was* a dear, sweet husband the evening before. He actually was concerned for my well being, but I was so charged with defending myself that I could not hear his words. They soared right over my head and out into the night.

While in the shower I was stunned into silence (pretty remarkable for me) by my lack of sensitivity — a quality I have lobbied Chuck for time and time again. The two by four in my own eye was feeling pretty heavy right about now. Later, on my prayer couch, God took me to my knees and stunned me into silence again by my own great need to drop the defenses and be quiet before Him. "Be still, Eileen, cease striving, let go, relax and KNOW that I AM GOD (Ps.46:10). Let loose of the defenses, let go of the pride, release the unbending spirit and lay them all at the foot of My Cross. You have no need to wear these chains. I wore them for you when I gave My life in your place. Drop them and be silenced by My love for you, My compassion for you, My forgiveness for all your sin now and forever."

Boy, God really knows how to get a girl's attention. Closing my Bible, I crept sheepishly up the stairs and into the hall where Chuck was selecting a tie to match his shirt. "Does this tie match?" he cautiously ventured. "Yeah, it's fine," I peeped, still looking sheepish. Somehow the words I longed to say took flight, except this time out of my brain, instead of out of my mouth as they had done the evening before.

I slowly walked into the kitchen to fix breakfast all the while God nudging me to go back to Chuck. Crawling out of my trench I approached Chuck who by this time was in the bathroom shaving. As I entered the doorway, he turned to look at me. From the look in his eyes, I knew he saw my white flag. I dropped my guns, which by now looked like tiny plastic water pistols! He listened as I delivered my verbal peace treaty. The surrender was complete. Both sides were reconciled and the world looked peacefully rosy again, at least for now. **I surrendered my right to defend myself and took on the RIGHT TO REMAIN SILENT.**

As this all too true account reveals it is often so difficult to admit when we are wrong or sometimes just simply bite our tongues and pray for godly wisdom. The Scriptures abound with the importance of practicing confession before God and before one another. How very vital confession is in a marriage relationship! Confession indicates to the other person that we are willing to humble ourselves and admit our faults (swallowing our enormous pride and choking on it if necessary).

Philippians 2:11 indicates that someday we each, whether Christian or non-Christian, will bow the knee before Jesus (the one who humbled himself on our behalf) and confess that He is Lord, to the glory of God the Father. We will agree with God that Jesus is worthy to be praised because of His work on the cross for us. We will either confess this truth gladly because we have already humbled ourselves on earth and made the glad confession, or we will be forced to confess the truth about the Lord Jesus.

I John 1:9 speaks of confessing our sins as Christians before God in order to restore our fellowship with Him. God's promise is that He is indeed "faithful and righteous to forgive us our sins and to cleanse us from all unrighteousness." Nothing can ever destroy our relationship with God once we have confessed the Lord Jesus as Saviour, but sin can certainly hinder our fellowship with the Father. Thus, it behooves us to clear the problem up as soon as we are aware of the offense.

Marriage With An Attitude

The marriage relationship is a picture of the Christian's relationship with God. Offenses toward one another in a marriage will not break the marriage bond, but they will certainly disrupt the blessed fellowship and friendship that we enjoy as partners and companions in this walk of life.

James 5:16 says, "Therefore, confess your sins to one another, and pray for one another, so that you may be healed. The effective prayer of a righteous man can accomplish much. "Healing in a relationship can take place when at least one partner steps forward to confess a wrong done. He/she is demonstrating humility and preference toward the other spouse. This move on the mate's part can open the door for forgiveness and restoration. Hopefully, the confessing partner will be met with open arms and a spirit of reconciliation.

Galatians 6:1 says, "....If a man is caught in any trespass, you who are spiritual, restore such a one in a spirit of gentleness, looking to yourself, lest you too be tempted." Both partners are in need of some confession to patch up the wounded relationship. This type of confession leads logically to forgiveness.

HOW CONFESSION LEADS TO FORGIVENESS

Forgiving each other supports the idea that we want reconciliation, peace and harmony rather than the prideful drive of having to be right. When we force the other person to be wrong we both lose. Choosing to forgive is behaving God's way, as it says in Ephesians 4:31-32. We are to forgive others "even as God for Christ's sake has forgiven you." To best understand forgiveness it is important to understand what forgiveness is NOT. For example, forgiveness is not conceding and giving in to what has happened. Forgiveness is also not condoning by agreeing that what happened was okay. Forgiveness is certainly not forgetting, which is the most misunderstood concept, because people have the mistaken notion that they must forget to forgive. "Just forgive and forget," is the common saying that is imbedded in our minds. The problem is that we will never forget. In fact, the stronger the emotional impact on us, the more the memory will be deeply imprinted in our brains.

Imprinting is that process in which the brain acts like a record. When the brain receives stimuli, the information is imprinted on the brain, similar to a needle repeatedly scratching a record eventually wears a groove on the surface. The scratch widens over time and destroys larger and larger parts of the record. So it is with the imprinting process in the brain. The more the negative issue is thought about, the deeper the groove develops. To this extent, that is all the brain can think about. Each repetitive thought is a new impression.

Let's face it — Our deepest hurts are thoughts we have thought about hundreds of times and the multiple impressions result in a dent the size of a canyon. This scientific phenomenon illustrates how difficult it is to forget. Also, remember that God's omniscience teaches us that He never forgets anything. So, we don't have to forget either. In fact, we can celebrate our memories when we deal with them God's way. The remembrance celebrates how we, with God's help, conquered the hurt and pain we originally experienced. We take our pains and hurts from others and choose to forgive. This benefits us significantly by allowing us to see how God can heal even our deepest pains and hurts. Many people are helped by writing a resolution letter that details what they have forgiven and how they have forgiven. This brings closure and can be reviewed at later times of testing.

When we forgive we break the cords that have bound us and kept us dancing the dance of anger. We break the strings that hold us like puppets. The people that hurt us are the puppet masters. The only way we can free ourselves from them is to forgive and thereby cut the puppet strings. Then we

Marriage With An Attitude

can learn to live our lives free from the anger, wrath, malice, slander or abusive speech that can dominate our lives if we choose not to forgive (Colosians 3:8).

Managing anger is crucial. When we hold on to anger we dance like puppets on strings. And who is holding the strings? The person with whom we are angry. The steps to anger management are twofold:

1. Tell the truth in all of its pain, ugliness, and gore.

A person might say, "I'm not angry; I just haven't forgiven him." That person is in denial. Another person might say, "The Bible doesn't allow me to be angry." This refutes Ephesians 4:26 which says, "Be angry, and yet do not sin; do not let the sun go down on your anger." This person reveals a lack of understanding of biblical teaching.

2. Choose to forgive the person.

Let this process begin immediately, because it may take some time to work it through. Consider the alternative—developing ulcers, colitis, stress and gastrointestinal distress just to name a few. Often, I receive referrals from physicians who can find no physical reason why the person is experiencing pain or distress. Later, we discover that unresolved anger is at the root. Resolving anger is one of the ways we can rejoice in the Lord and learn to be content in whatever circumstances we find ourselves (Philippians 4:4,11). In short, managing anger lets us enjoy life more. Then we are ready to stay current by not letting the sun go down on our anger (Ephesians 4:26).

Sometimes forgiveness is difficult because we want revenge. The following story told by Charles Lowery, the pastor of Hoffmantown Church in Albuquerque, N.M., illustrates this point in a somewhat humorous way.

Chuck & Eileen Rife

A man was thumbing through the classifieds. He saw an ad he couldn't believe: Almost new Jag, loaded, $200. Thinking it was a misprint he called the number. Sure enough, the almost brand-new Jaguar was loaded and only had 300 miles on it. The woman verified the price and said the first one to her house would get the car.

He was the first one there. He looked at the car, which appeared to be in mint condition, and thought there must be something wrong with it. He asked. "Ma'am, is it really $200?"

She paused and then she said, "That might be too much. I'll let you have it for $99.50."

He said, "I'll take it, but I'd feel guilty if I didn't tell you it's worth $50,000. Why would you sell it to me for only $99.50?"

She said, "My husband ran away with his secretary last week. He just sent me a telegram from Hawaii telling me to sell the Jag and send him the money. That's exactly what I'm going to do!"

After 34 years of marriage, Sheila discovered that John was having an affair with a co-worker. She immediately sent him packing. John found himself on his parents' doorstep midnight of April 1, 1997. Sheila received counsel from her pastor, who asked her if she would consider forgiving John. When she asked the pastor why she should forgive her wayward husband, the pastor referred to Ephesians 4:31-32. He said that regardless of whether the marriage continued she would need to forgive John, to completely grieve the loss and go forward with her life. The pastor also reminded her that this would help her assist her children, Adam, age four, and Sally, age eight, through their own grieving process.

Marriage With An Attitude

Sheila decided she would be willing to enter into counseling with John. That is when I first met them. At that point, John was willing and ready to sever all relationship with the other woman and very much wanted to see the marriage restored. Being back at home with his parents, John was riddled with advice from them that contradicted what they were learning through the counseling. I soon became aware that John would need to leave his father and mother before he would be able to appropriately cleave unto his wife, as Genesis 2:24 directs. So, John moved out of his parents' home into an apartment. He limited communication with his parents and joined a Promise Keeper's group at his church.

After two months of consistently attending church and counseling sessions with Sheila, she was ready to forgive him and let him move back home. Both of them understood that trust needed to continue to be earned, although forgiveness had been granted. He allowed her to call him multiple times throughout the day to check on his whereabouts. He voluntarily called her to discuss his whereabouts, which was easy since they had caller-ID. They began dating each other weekly and established a time for family devotions. They also continued regular church attendance, along with counseling for another two months. At the end of this time, they celebrated their reunion with a recommitment ceremony at their church.

A year later, Sheila indicated that she was almost thankful that the affair had happened because the effort they had expended in the aftermath of the affair had resulted in a better marriage. Sheila and John's experience is a good example of how confession can lead to forgiveness and restoration in a marriage.

But what if the hurt and anger are so blinding that one or both partners cannot see beyond them to focus on reconciliation? Allowing anger to go unchecked in our lives is like a teenager who wears a mask to hide a blemish. Wearing a mask merely aggravates the problem because the mask is more noticeable than the blemish would ever be. Anger is like the pimple. The hurt and loss represent the mask. The pimple will grow and fester if not properly treated; so will the anger. The mask may make a good showing, but it really does not solve the root of the problem.

During the Master's Final, golf pro, Sam Snead missed an easy putt that caused him to lose the match because he refused to control his anger. He was angry at his competitor's insistence about following a technical rule. He let this anger get the better of him, which led to his loss. We need to make sure we do not let anger control us. Again, the way to do this is to CHOOSE to forgive.

I have always been intrigued by the truth of Henry Wadsworth Longfellow's brief, but exacting poem entitled *"Retribution."*

> ***Though the mills of God grind slowly,***
> ***Yet they grind exceeding small;***
> ***Though with patience He stands waiting,***
> ***With exactness grinds He all.***

I see the marital union as one of God's mills. Learning to confess and to forgive is a grinding process that God requires of His children in order that we might be conformed to the image of His Son. Our heavenly Father stands patiently waiting as He works His plan through our lives. He will not miss the smallest detail, but will crush and grind until He has shaped and formed us to perfection. This grinding will last a lifetime and will one day be complete in heaven. Praise God!

God knows that the marriage relationship is one of the best ways to mold us after His image as we work through our daily battles of communication, confession and forgiveness. It's

Marriage With An Attitude

getting up off our faces and beginning a new day again. In their book, *A Rainbow of Hope,* Billy and Janice Hughey quote a writer who once said, "Making marriage work is like running a farm. You have to start all over again each morning."

Learning to confess and forgive means confronting the problem head-on and then learning to move past the offense to never bring it up again. As the Scriptures express, "Love covers a multitude of sin." We would do well to practice this in our marriages, to "forget what lies behind, reach forward to what lies ahead and press on toward the goal for the prize of the upward call of God in Christ Jesus" (Philippians 3:13b-14).

God forgives us, so we too as Christians should forgive our mates. I am reminded of this truth when I recall an incident that happened shortly after Chuck and I were married. I hate to iron. Ask Chuck! He'll tell you ironing has never been at the top of my most wanted activities. When we were first married, I was forced to iron a favorite blouse my sister had made for me. Forced, simply because even I could not bring myself to wear it in its present crumpled condition. So I set about pressing. I didn't realize I had pushed the temperature setting to wool instead of cool — which was required for the sheer material with which I was working. As I dutifully pressed along, I lifted the iron to begin another section and to my horror, I caught sight of a huge scorch print on the sleeve of my blouse. I was devastated. My doom was sealed. I was right all along. My homemaking skills were a disaster. Maybe I couldn't pull this thing called marriage off after all.

I took the blouse off the board and crept sheepishly into the other room where Chuck was busily studying. As I revealed the blouse with the damaged sleeve tears flooded my eyes and Chuck knew the situation was critical — at least in my mind. He gave a little chuckle (no pun intended), took me in his arms, looked into my eyes and reassured me our marriage wasn't over simply because I blundered on one blouse. He loved me anyhow. I felt better and set about thinking how I might redeem the little mishap. I decided to cut the sleeves and make short bell-sleeves. I must have worn that blouse a couple of years after that incident.

Whenever I think of pressing clothing (which I still avoid as much as possible), I am reminded of Paul's words in Phillipians 3:12b, "I press on in order that I may lay hold of that for which also I was laid hold of by Christ Jesus." When I see a scorch mark on my spiritual garment, my bridegroom, Jesus, looks at me, lifts up my face, gazes into my eyes and says, "I love you; I chose you; I died for you and rose again for you in order to clothe you with the perfect, spotless robe of My righteousness — no stains, no wrinkles and definitely no scorch marks. "Oh, your garment may seem disfigured from your earthly point of view, but from where I sit (in the heavenlies) 'you look marvelous'! And someday when I take you to heaven to be with Me forever, you will see fully that I was right all along."

Let's face it, dear reader, you and your spouse have plenty of scorch marks, but Jesus' reminder to all of us today is keep pressing on, inspite of mistakes, seeming failure, outright sin or foolish blunders — take the mess to Jesus and claim His deep love, total forgiveness and absolute acceptance for you. Lay hold of these truths that are provided in His person and you will begin to see yourself and your mate the way Jesus sees you. The more you understand Jesus' total love and acceptance for you, the easier you will find it to confess your faults to your spouse and forgive him/her when needed.

Look over the practical helps at the end of this chapter. Do a study of the Scripture passages and make your own list of positive affirmation statements that you can review each day, perhaps several times a day. This practice is part of God's renewal process for your mind spoken of in Romans 12:1-2.

Marriage With An Attitude

Get into the habit of positive imprinting and put some healthy grooves into that brain of yours!

Learn to confess who you are in Christ, but also honestly deal with your faults, confessing them to your spouse when necessary. Remember to always be ready to forgive in return. Learn to cuddle that accused spouse and receive him back into full fellowship. Read Perry Tanksley's insightful poem often as you go about your daily lives.

Mere love is not enough
To make a marriage great.
It takes the love of God
To be a winsome mate.

It takes God's love and grace
To make a marriage, heaven-
Grace that forgives and loves
Seventy times seven.
—Perry Tanksley © Used by permission

PRACTICAL HELPS

Marriage With An Attitude
LEARNING TO MAKE THE GOOD CONFESSION

BEFORE GOD

1. Understand that if you have received the Lord Jesus as your own personal Saviour, you stand before God completely forgiven, totally accepted and righteous (Eph. 1:3-14).

2. Understand that you still walk in the flesh and will sin daily, so learn to confess your sin to God as soon as the Holy Spirit makes you conscious of your wrong-doing (1 John 1:9).

3. Turn to Galatians 5:22-23 and see the fruit of the Spirit.

4. Take a clean sheet of paper or if you prefer, you may write in the spaces provided here. List the fruit of the Spirit down the left side of your paper. Beside each word, write one thing that would show you doing God's will in a way that you currently are not doing. You may choose to fit it into the following format. In so doing, you are making the good confession of who God is making you to be.

LOVE: I, Chuck Rife, now thank God for making me a loving person as I daily <u>communicate with Eileen.</u>

JOY: I, (supply your name), now thank God for making me a joyful person as I daily_____.

PEACE: I,_____, now thank God for making me a peaceful person as I daily_____.

PATIENCE: I,_____, now thank God for making me a patient person as I daily_____.

—62—

KINDNESS: I,_____, now thank God for making me a kind person as I daily_____.

GOODNESS: I, _____, now thank God for making me a good person as I daily_____.

FAITHFULNESS: I,_____,now thank God for making me a faithful person as I daily_____.

GENTLENESS: I,_____, now thank God for making me a gentle person as I daily_____.

SELF-CONTROL: I,_____, now thank God for making me a controlled person as I daily_____.

5. Repeat each affirmation or confession 3 times onto a tape or disc, even the Bible verses. Repetition is the key to learning. Repeat the affirmations until the tape is full.

6. If you desire, include a relaxing instrumental music background onto your tape.

7. Pick a daily time and place to listen to your tape. The car is a great place. You can be doing other things and not actively listening. Listen at least 30 minutes a day.

8. Be patient with yourself. Do not expect immediate changes. Laugh at yourself. You will get past the initial uncomfortable feelings. Remember, you are applying, in a practical way, Phillipians 4:8 "Think on these things."

9. Rejoice that you are agreeing with God as you confess your affirmations.

Marriage With An Attitude

10. For further study, use the following Biblical truths about Christians to confess what God says about you as His child. Repeat steps 5-9.

BIBLE TRUTHS ABOUT CHRISTIANS

Truth	Reference
I am blessed.	Deut. 28:1-14
I am overtaken with blessings.	Deut. 28:2
I am the head and not the tail, I am above only and not beneath.	Deut. 28:13
I am the apple of my Father's eye.	Ps. 17:8

I am fearfully and wonderfully made.	Ps. 139:14
I am thought of often by God.	Ps. 139:17-18
I am loved with an everlasting love.	Jer. 31:3
I am the salt of the earth.	Matt. 5:13

I am the light of the world.	Matt. 5:14
I am a child of God, part of His family.	John 1:12
I have everlasting life.	John 6
I am set free.	John 8:31-33

I have abundant life.	John 10:10
I know God's voice.	John 10:14
I am a disciple of Christ and love others.	John 13:34
I shall do even greater works than Christ.	John 14:12

I am part of the true vine, a channel (branch) of His (Christ's) life.	John 15:1,5
I am Christ's friend.	John 15:15
I am chosen and appointed by Christ to be fruit.	John 15:16
I am one with other believers in Christ.	John 17:21-23

I am a saint.	Rom.1:7, Eph1:1, 1Cor.1:2
I am dead to sin.	Rom. 6:2, 11
I am a slave to righteousness.	Rom. 6:18
I am enslaved to God.	Rom. 6:22

I live by the law of the Holy Spirit.	Rom. 8:2
I am a Son of God. He is my spiritual father.	Rom.8:14, 15 Gal.3:26, 4:6
I am a joint-heir with Christ sharing His inheritance with Him.	Rom. 8:17
I am more than a conqueror.	Rom. 8:37

Marriage With An Attitude

I am in Christ Jesus by His doing.	I Cor. 1:30
I have the mind of Christ.	I Cor. 2:16
I am a temple (home) of God.	
His Spirit dwells in me.	I Cor. 3:16; 6:19
I am joined (united) to the Lord and am one spirit with Him.	I Cor. 5:17

I am the temple of the Holy Spirit.	1 Cor. 6:19
I am a member (part) of Christ's body.	1 Cor. 12:27
I always triumph in Christ.	2 Cor. 2:14
I am a new creation (new person).	2 Cor. 5:17

I am raised up in Christ & seated in heaven.	Col. 2:12
I am hidden with Christ in God.	Col. 3:3
I am an expression of the life of Christ, because He is my life.	Col. 3:4
I am chosen of God, holy and dearly loved.	Col. 3:12

I am chosen & dearly loved by God.	I Thess. 1:4
I am a son of light.	I Thess. 5:5
I am called of God.	2 Tim. 1:9
I am holy & a partaker of a heavenly calling.	Heb. 3:1

I am a partaker of Christ...I share in His life.	Heb. 3:14
I am the first fruits among His creation.	James 1:18
I am God's child for I am born again of the incorruptible seed of the Word of God, which lives & abides forever.	I Pet. 1:23

Chuck & Eileen Rife

I am one of God's living stones and am being built up (in Christ) as a spiritual house.	I Pet. 2:5

I am a chosen race, a royal priesthood, a holy nation, a people for God's own possession to proclaim His excellencies.	I Pet. 2:9-10
I am an alien and stranger to this world that I temporarily live in.	I Pet. 2:11
I am healed by the wounds of Jesus.	I Pet. 2:24
I am an enemy of the devil.	I Pet. 5:8

I am a partaker of His divine nature.	2 Pet. 1:4
I am now a child of God. I will resemble Christ when He returns.	I Jn. 3:1,2
I possess the Greater One in me because greater is He in me than he who is in the world.	I Jn. 4:4
I have overcome the world.	I Jn. 5:4

I am born of God and the evil one (the devil) cannot touch me.	I Jn. 5:18
I am victorious.	Rev. 21:7

Marriage With An Attitude
LEARNING TO MAKE THE GOOD CONFESSION

BEFORE MY SPOUSE

1. First of all, determine if you have sinned against God only or also against your spouse. When the Holy Spirit convicts, reproves and corrects in righteousness, do what He says!

2. Is there anything I wake-up about at night concerning my marriage?

3. Is there anything I need to confess or forgive in my marriage?

4. Manage your anger according to Ephesians 4:26.

(a) Tell the truth about your anger and lack of forgiveness.

(b) Choose to forgive your spouse.

(c) Never bring up the offense again to your mate or anyone else.

A man in love is incomplete until he has married; then He's finished.

Rachel A. Park

3

ATTITUDE OF THANKSGIVING
"Telling the Truth"
♥

HOLIDAY PARTIES, you've been there — maybe to more than one. You know, seasonal mood enhancers, warm family gatherings, the energetic laughter of friends, the ever increasing waistline, a cup of eggnog or cider by a crackling fire, another helping of Aunt Gertrude's fruit cake, the romantic glow of candlelight. In short — **the making of a memory!**

After the curtain closes on all the holiday parties, and the curtain rises on the still, quiet coldness of January, I receive one more party invitation. I tear open the envelope and there written on the inside card is the following message.

YOU ARE INVITED TO A JANUARY PITY PARTY.
BRING A FRIEND AND COME PREPARED TO
WALLOW IN YOUR TROUBLES.

YOURS TRULY,
SATAN

RSVP

This particular invite is quite attractive with the RSVP gold-embossed on the bottom. I know I have a choice to make.

Marriage With An Attitude

As I was flipping through my spiritual journal, I came across an entry I made last year in January. My writing served as a reminder to avoid some of the same pitfalls that await me year after year, one of which is attending Satan's annual pity party. My tendency every January is to close up shop, pull within myself, bemoan my ill lot in life and wait it out until spring. Don't get me wrong, the winter months can serve as a healthy time of reflection, but excessive introspection can lead to depression.

Here is what I wrote on January 26, 1998.

I just glanced at my previous entry "JOY in the mundane." Ah! I know I need to experience joy now, but it's JANUARY and I feel low. I've wanted to run away since Christmas — pull within myself and not come out for awhile. Well, that's pretty much what I have done, pulled within myself and away from others, especially Chuck. He's beginning to notice my cool distance, enough to remark about it.

Sometimes I wonder how on earth our marriage can survive. At times it seems like we're hanging by a thread, so fragile. The fact is **MARRIAGE IS FRAGILE!** We're fragile. Life's fragile. Relationships of all sorts must be nurtured and handled with great care. I haven't been handling Chuck with much care the last few weeks. I asked him yesterday how I could help make things different. He offered two suggestions:

1. Share my feelings daily, either verbally or in writing. Don't stuff everything inside.

2. Don't say anything negative, either write it down or find a friend to share with. In other words, go heavy on the positive affirmation and lighten up on the husband bashing. "A good word fitly spoken" achieves greater results than critical words. Heap on the praise and

encouragement! "Let no unwholesome word proceed from your mouth, but only such a word as is good for edification according to the need of the moment, that it may give grace to those who hear" (Ephesians 4:29).

3. (I think I can add a third). Respond to his attempts at affection, especially the "hello's" and "good-byes." A ten second hug works wonders. So, get up off the couch and relate, even if only for ten seconds.

Can't I just be irritable and grouchy, Lord? I realize You have me in a corner. I'm squirming, I want my own way, but I'm miserable in it. I'm so full of myself. I want joy, but I am not willing to take the step of faith to get out of my pit to receive it. If I begin to ACT joyfully and respond kindly to Chuck, I will indeed be joyful. Obedience breeds joy!

I know I must respond. I choose to be joyful. I determine in my heart to encourage Chuck today, respond to him and initiate communication. I choose to climb out of my pit for the benefit of another.

As I look around I get the impression I am not alone at this party. It is so easy to fall into a pit of our own making, succumbing to the temptation to wallow there until other people change or circumstances improve. We each have the opportunity to choose daily what kind of party we will attend — whether it is a pity party or a praise party. You can determine now, with God's help, to pull yourself out one step at a time. Write down a plan of action, pray daily for the grace to follow it and keep climbing, with eyes that intently focus on Jesus.

Philippians 2 indicates that Jesus was in the worst of circumstances while here on earth. Not only had He already willingly laid aside many of His attributes in order to identify with us as human beings, but He also

Marriage With An Attitude

subjected Himself to abuses of every kind and misunderstandings, even by His own earthly family. But inspite of all this and yes, even in the midst of all of this, He was thankful, because He knew God's plan of redemption was being carried out and that it would impact millions of lives for time to come.

Hebrews 12:2 says that Jesus "endured the cross, despising the shame because of the JOY set before Him." He had the ability to look beyond the horror of the cross because He knew that the cross was a point in history, a limited span in time that would soon be over and never repeated again. He took joy in the fact that He was delivering millions from an eternity in hell and ushering them into eternal bliss with the Father.

I believe Jesus models before us a significant principle of life here on earth. At times horrible events occur over which we have no control, but each event is merely a point in time, a rather insignificant point in time compared to eternity. If we can train ourselves to look beyond the momentary affliction to our everlasting reward we will most surely discover JOY. Also, when we realize that our heavenly Father is using these momentary light afflictions to shape us after the character of His dear Son, we can learn to bear up under hard times. Hebrews 12:11 says, "all discipline <u>for the moment</u> seems not to be joyful but sorrowful; yet to those who have been trained by it, afterwards it yields the peaceful fruit of righteousness." It helps to compare our momentary afflictions with eternity. Ecclesiastes 4:11 says, "God has set eternity in our hearts." Imagine yourself one million years into your forever bliss in heaven. You look back at this moment in time and chuckle at its insignificance because you see it in the light of eternity. You can see clearly how it helped you mature.

Chuck & Eileen Rife

The Apostle Paul was no stranger to life's afflictions. Acts 16 is only one example of his many confrontations with peril and persecution at the hands of those who were blinded to his gospel message. Having been arrested for preaching the gospel and thrown into prison, Paul and Silas sit chained to a prison wall. Do we find them crying and complaining? No. Rather, they are rejoicing and singing praises to God. Exactly what Paul admonishes each one of us to do in Philippians chapter 4. Even as he wrote this cheerful epistle he was imprisoned. So you see, Paul was not speaking to us out of mere theory. He actually experienced what he was teaching about. Paul had learned the secret of contentment in whatever circumstances he found himself. Our marriages may not be all we desire them to be, but can we, like Paul, learn to find contentment in our union, even while praying and working to make it better? I believe it is possible.

Our world abounds with lies. Here are a few you might have heard. I will respect you in the morning. The check is in the mail. The delivery is on the truck. I'm from the IRS and I'm here to help you. Finally, you can experience MARITAL CONTENTMENT without following the principles found in Philippians chapter 4.

Have there been times when you felt like you were in way over your head in your marriage relationship? You may think, "Why even try anymore? Is it really worth it? Why can't I simply take the easy way out like so many others and throw in the towel?"

Before joining the Royal Canadian Mounted Police, applicants are given an exam. A would-be constable was given a hypothetical situation. He arrives at a gas explosion to find numerous casualties. He notices a drunk driver whom he recognizes as the wife of a senior official. A nearby woman starts to give birth. Someone is drowning in a canal, while a fight breaks out which could

Marriage With An Attitude

result in loss of life and damage. The question to answer is "In a few words, describe what you would do." One applicant faced with this situation wrote, "I would remove my uniform and mingle with the crowd."

Have your marital responsibilities ever made you feel this way? You think, maybe I could just strip away this cloak of matrimony and be a free agent again. Contentment is a choice. Philippians 4:4-5 tells us how we can choose contentment in our marriages. Verse 4 says to "rejoice in the Lord always." Proverbs 17:22 says, "a joyful heart is good medicine." Many people think that Norman Vincent Peale, who himself was a preacher for about 50 years, was the originator of positive thinking. Actually, Paul, David, and Jesus beat him to it, as Acts and Psalms indicate.

Several thoughts emerge as we consider this idea of contentment.

➢ Joy or contentment is based on faith in God, not ideal circumstances. In Acts 16:16, Paul sang out of faith, not ideal circumstances. Don't think for one minute that he and Silas felt good chained to a dingy, dank, cold prison wall. We can change how we feel by choosing to act differently. One of the biggest mistakes I have made in our twenty-three years of marriage was when I insisted Eileen take a Dale Carnegie course! I thought she'd benefit from it. But she never did learn to enjoy it, so it was counterproductive. But one lesson in the course illustrates the point that we can change how we feel by choosing to act differently. One evening as the tired participants arrived from their homes and jobs, the instructor guided the room of 80-100 people to follow him in saying "Boy, am I enthusiastic!" As you can imagine the instructor was not impressed with the response. So, he told the group to do it again and this time if there was anyone that did not convince him that they were excited they would have to come in front of the entire group and say the phrase until everyone was convinced. This time everyone enthusiastically and in unison yelled, "Boy, am I enthusiastic!" Immediately, there was a buzz in the room, excitement and energy that they had not previously felt. What happened? Because they had acted enthusiastic by actively participating, they <u>felt</u> more enthusiastic. **WE CAN CHANGE HOW WE FEEL BY ACTING DIFFERENTLY.** We need to be more childlike and spontaneous in our relationship with one another and stop making everything a major issue. Learn to lighten up and feel the stress drain from your relationship together.

➤ You see what you are prepared to see. Warren Wiersbe once said, "What the heart loves, the eyes will see. "How many of you enjoy fishing? How many despise it? This fish story takes place on Lake Michigan, two miles off the coast of Loudington, Michigan. My dad, two brothers, Vern and Ron and I (Chuck) were on a charter boat with Nate, our guide. Nate placed about 10 poles around the back and sides of our vessel and began to slowly trawl. Every once in a while Nate would jump up, run to a pole, set the hook in the fish's mouth and then hand us the pole to reel in the fish. Call that fishing if you want, but it seemed rather odd to me. My point in telling you this story is that Nate was the only one who ever saw the line go down in the water. All my brothers, my dad, and I ever saw was the backside of Nate running to retrieve the poles. He had that trained eye. He was prepared to see the lines move.

In the same way, Jesus was prepared to see beyond the cross to the resurrection and to us today, being able to experience forgiveness of sins and a right relationship with God. Nothing expresses Jesus' attitude better than during The Last Supper with his disciples. He chose to sing in Hebrew, the Hillel, a collection of songs that

Marriage With An Attitude

expressed His joy in the day the Lord had made (Psalm118:24).

So, too, we as marriage partners need to be prepared to rejoice and see the good in each other. We need to view one another as a unique gift from the Father, a treasure to be highly prized. **LEARN TO CATCH EACH OTHER BEING GOOD AND OFFER A WORD OF PRAISE!**

➢ What you see is what you get. Ephesians 4:29 and Proverbs 12:25 express the thought that "a good word makes the heart glad." How many ways can you say, "Good job, way to go!" My missionary friend, Steve Richardson, taught me that in Australia they say, "GOOD ON YA, MATE!"

The preacher on the popular TV program, *Dr. Quinn-Medicine Woman*, related the following story from his pulpit on one particular episode:

Long ago, in a small rural community, a king brought his infant child before his subjects. Before he left he informed the leaders that he had switched his baby with one of the babies in the community nursery. The king said he would be back to check on his child. The leaders were very concerned because they did not know which child was the king's. And they wanted to be sure to take special care of his child, lest he be displeased on his return. So, they developed a plan. They decided to treat all of the children as the king's child. And so they did. Years later when all of the children had grown up the king returned to the community. But now there were schools, hospitals, cultural centers and places of worship. One elderly woman approached the king and said, "It was my child wasn't it?" The king answered and said, "No, it was all of the children." The king had only said he had switched his child. But because all of the people treated their own children royally, as if they were the king's, they all turned

Chuck & Eileen Rife

out royally. Because the people saw royalty in their children that's exactly what they got. WHAT YOU SEE IS WHAT YOU GET. So, rejoice by faith!

Philippians 4:5 encourages us to let our patience shine through. How do you respond to slow drivers, to disobedience and to other people's mistakes? Roger Anderson said, "Accept that some days you're the pigeon, and some days you're the statue." To be patient with your spouse, you must learn to be patient with yourself. Often the things that bug us most about our mates are the very things we can't tolerate in ourselves. Be aware that we are all in a process of growth. Again, learn to lighten up and laugh at yourself more. Remember we are each on different levels of development, even as adults. Be there for one another.

David Mains tells about his friend whose son developed an avid interest in baseball. My friend wasn't interested in baseball at all. But one summer he took his son to see every major league team play one game. The trip took over six weeks and cost a great deal of money, but it became a powerful bonding experience in their relationship. My friend was asked on his return, "Do you like baseball that much?"

"No," he replied, "but I like my son that much."

Do you cherish your spouse enough to express interest in his or her hobbies, goals, etc.? I have developed a liking for golf, and although Eileen does not share my eagerness, she asks how my game went when I return home and encourages me to play with "the guys" when I can. I reciprocate by showing interest in her newfound desire to learn to play the guitar. There are many ways to show you care. Caring does not always mean you must become actively involved in the other person's pursuit. It may just mean you show interest and encouragement.

Marriage With An Attitude

Philippians 4:6 reminds us to pray with thanksgiving. God has lavished us with His indescribable gifts, one of which is your spouse! When we are thanking God for all He has done for us and all He is doing, it is much easier to trust Him to continue to work on our behalf.

BELIEVE THREE THINGS:
1.) God is.
2.) God loves us.
3.) God has a wonderful plan for our lives and is committed to assisting us to find it and implement it.

Therefore, nothing that happens to us can deter us, unless we let it. Joseph said to his brothers, who sold him into slavery, "You meant it for evil, but God meant it for good"(Gen. 50:20). Joseph believed that "all things work together for good to those who love God and are called according to His purpose," as Romans 8:28 teaches.

The way to conquer your anxiety about your marriage or anything for that matter is not by asking God to take the fear away, but by thanking Him BY FAITH to act on your behalf. My dad taught me this lesson every time I had to play the trumpet in front of a group. He would say, "It's okay to have butterflies. Just make the butterflies fly in formation!" I have always appreciated his advice. It works. I'm living proof. I understand that there is a book entitled, *Feel the Fear and Do It Anyway*. The way I like to express it is *FEEL THE FEAR, BUT DO THE GOD-HONORING BEHAVIOR ANYWAY.*

Some key points to consider are:

1. It is hard to be thankful and anxious at the same time. Choose one.

2. By faith make a thankful list daily. Praise God for each item. We take a lot for granted especially each other.

3. Any request that is consistent with God's character will be answered. Psalm 37:4, one of my favorite promises, says, "Delight yourself in the Lord and He will give you the desires of your heart." The key is make sure your focus is where it belongs — on God.

Moving on to Philippians 4:8, Paul admonishes us to think correctly. In order to produce work elephants, Asians break the will of these huge creatures by a process begun in infanthood. The baby elephant is tied to a wooden stake, unable to break free. So conditioned is the little elephant to remain stationary that even when grown, he remains at the stake even though he is strong enough to now break free. Many of us are this way. We are so conditioned by our negative memories that we let them rule our present lives, even though the reality is that we can now break free from the stake. We do not have to wallow in failure, inability and powerlessness. 2 Cor. 10:5 exhorts us to "bring into captivity every thought to the obedience of Christ."

In Numbers 11:1-9, the Israelites complained because of the manna God provided. All we ever see is this disgusting manna, they lamented day after day. O BE CAREFUL LITTLE EYES WHAT YOU SEE! Attitude determines whether we see with eyes of gratitude or eyes of disgust.

Make a GOOD THOUGHTS LIST. Using the guidelines in the practical helps section following this chapter, take a few moments and jot down under each category of Phil. 4:8 some things that you know are TRUE, HONORABLE, RIGHT and so on. Learning the verse is a beginning, but actually DOING the verse can change your attitude and help you experience more joy

Marriage With An Attitude

and contentment in your marriage. Use the good thoughts list daily for one week and you will find yourself looking for the positives more and more often in your life. Your mate will notice a difference and will enjoy being around you.

Phil.4: 9 exhorts us to ACT APPROPRIATELY. Paul wanted the Philippians to PUT OFF the old ways of living and PUT ON the new, godly ways of living. A good cross-reference study on "putting off" and "putting on" is found in Colossians 3:8 & 12. Paul was not satisfied for the Philippian believers to just know the truth. He wanted them to DO THE TRUTH. He wanted them to take everything that they had learned and received and APPLY IT. He wanted them to take what they had heard from him and seen him do and FOLLOW HIS EXAMPLE. Paul would have been an excellent spokesperson for NIKE! JUST DO IT!

We need to be careful not to sit, soak and sour in church. Our oldest daughter, Rachel, was in Israel in 1999 with her Bible college class. One of the highlights of her trip was floating in the Dead Sea. She was able to do this because of all the salt. The sea is "dead" because there is no outlet. **Be sure you have an outlet for what God teaches you.** A client once told me that she was listening to testimonies in a group I was leading and she realized that the only difference between her and others that had experienced breakthroughs in their lives was that they had DONE what God had directed them to do and she had NOT.

Key points to consider:

1. We need to let God's Word into our lives, but we also need to let it out behaviorally by doing His will.

2. We must DO THE TRUTH we know for it to make a positive difference in our lives.

Chuck & Eileen Rife

God's peace mentioned in Philippians 4:7-9 becomes more real to us when we practice what God teaches us. When our minds are focused or stayed on Him, we experience perfect peace. When we seek His kingdom first, rather than our own selfish desires, He provides peace.

Horatio G. Spafford, after his only son died, lost his real estate in the great Chicago fire and his four daughters at sea, by God's amazing grace penned the great words of the well-known hymn, *"It is Well With My Soul."* How could he say that? Obviously, he had learned the secret of contentment and of keeping his focus clearly on God alone.

Paul knew how to abound and be abased. He was neither intimidated nor overwhelmed by money, possessions or prestige. He knew how to manage it when he had it and how to manage without it. His contentment was not contingent upon his station or circumstances in life. Verse 11 clearly reflects Paul's attitude. To enjoy God, do the math. Verses 4+5+6+8+9=verses 11,13,7,9,19.

To be content, we must live in the present, refusing to dwell on the hurts of the past or worry about the uncertainties of the future. When I was a little girl, I used to long for the next age. When I was ten, I wanted to be fifteen; when I was fifteen, I wanted to be twenty. Somehow I thought that there must be some magical age out there when life would be perfect. Well, I arrived at each age only to discover that there is no perfect age or perfect life. Each stage has its difficulties and hurts. Through this realization God forced my hand and caused me to see that the only way to live a contented life is to live in the present.

Materialism can be a distraction to contentment. Proverbs 23:4 encourages us not to weary ourselves to

Marriage With An Attitude

gain riches. Andrew Carnegie was asked how many more millions he needed to be content. He replied, "Just one more."

"Relish the moment" is a good motto when considering this issue of contentment, especially when coupled with Psalm 118:24, "This is the day which the Lord has made; we will rejoice and be glad in it."

If you are in mid-life, you may experience some interesting challenges to marital harmony with physical changes, kids leaving home and possible job changes.

Someone wrote humorously, that you know you've reached middle age when:

1. You know all the answers, but no one asks you the questions.

2. You are too tired to work, but too broke to quit.

3. Your work is less fun and your fun is more work.

4. Your narrow waist and your broad mind have changed places.

5. You have more hair growing in your ears than on your head.

6. You read the obituary column every day to see if anyone your age has died.
     (Anonymous)

Another person has this perspective on being middle aged:

When I was a child, I desperately wanted to be older. When I was 8, I couldn't wait to be 12. When I was 12, I

Chuck & Eileen Rife

wanted to be 16. And when I was 16, I wanted to be 20. And when I was 30, I wanted to be 20. I stepped on the accelerator of life until I reached age 21. Then when I hit the brakes, I discovered they didn't work and the accelerator was stuck.

(Anonymous)

Make sure you are living for things that will stand the test of time. Things that will come forth as gold, silver and precious metals, rather than be burned up like wood, hay and stubble. Your marriage is one of those costly, precious metals. Don't trade it in on stubble.

In verse 13, Paul reminds us of God's power. This is a strong Biblical affirmation. We can do whatever God's will is for us. His will is always good, acceptable and perfect. Giving our marriages the best of ourselves is always God's will. Be encouraged to keep on keeping on in that pursuit!

Finally, in verse 19, Paul reminds us that God is the source of all our needs. Whether we need financial assistance, wisdom, patience, whatever. He is there to meet that need.

I once counseled a man in his mid-forties who claimed he could not find one thing to be thankful for; thus he lived a life of continual defeat. His healing began with thankfulness. I am reminded of a prayer that one of my English professors in college would open the class with every morning, "God, help us remember that You are closer than the air we breathe and closer than our hands and feet." I did not realize at the time that these words came from one of Alfred Lord Tennyson's poems. Tennyson certainly knew something of the reality of God's presence. **That knowledge alone is worthy of thanksgiving!**

Marriage With An Attitude

One of Satan's most effective tools in crippling our lives and marriages is discouragement. Discouragement can't thrive where thanksgiving dwells. Hannah Smith, in her timeless and practical book, *The Christian's Secret of a Happy Life*, relates this story.

Satan called together a council of his servants to consult how they might make a good man sin. One evil spirit started up and said, "I will make him sin."

"How will you do it?" asked Satan.

"I will set before him the pleasures of sin," was the reply; "I will tell him of its delights and the rich rewards it brings."

"Ha," said Satan, "that will not do; he has tried it, and knows better than that."

Then another spirit started up and said, "I will make him sin."

"What will you do?" asked Satan.

"I will tell him of the pains and sorrows of virtue. I will show him that virtue has no delights, and brings no rewards."

"Ha, no!" exclaimed Satan, "that will not do at all; for he has tried it, and knows that wisdom's ways are ways of pleasantness and all her paths are peace."

"Well," said another imp, starting up, "I will undertake to make him sin."

"And what will you do?" asked Satan again.

"I will discourage his soul," was the short reply.

"Ha, that will do," cried Satan, "that will do it! We shall conquer him now." And they did."

An old writer says, "All discouragement is from the devil." I wish every Christian would just take this as a pocket-piece, and never forget it. We must flee from discouragement as we would from sin.

Chuck & Eileen Rife

It can never be said too often that **DISCOURAGEMENT CAN'T THRIVE WHERE THANKSGIVING DWELLS.** Purpose in your heart to practice cheerful thankfulness today. Sit down and write out a list of all the ways God has blessed your life and marriage.

A few weeks ago, Chuck was asked to speak at a church on this very topic of thankfulness. He asked me to share an article on this topic during his treatise of Philippians 4:4-13. Before we left that morning for church, I received a phone call from my mother reporting that my dad had gone into the hospital with what the doctors thought was a mild stroke. I was shaken and immediately wanted to get into the car and drive to Tennessee to be with my mom and dad. One of my sisters lived close by my parents and was caring for them adequately, so as I came to my senses, I realized I was not to go just yet. Not being there with them was difficult, however, and I wondered how I would get up before the group and speak about joy and thankfulness. I felt anything but joy just then.

When we arrived at the church I sensed an immediate reception and warmth that began to erode some of my misgivings. As the service commenced and I sat listening to various people share prayer requests, I realized I was in the midst of the Body of Christ, simply hurting together, having all things in common. I felt a united camaraderie as we shared our concerns.

Never is it easy to get up in front of people, but as I walked to the podium, I experienced a reassuring calmness that I was exactly where God wanted me to be at that moment. He was giving me a chance to be a minister of joy in the midst of a stressful situation. I was able to share the following story with renewed vigor and

Marriage With An Attitude

confidence that I was really encouraging specific ones through my words.

Have you ever noticed how free and spontaneous a little child is at play or in any area of life for that matter? I remember when our girls emerged from the womb to embark on their earthly journey. They had no inhibitions in their young bodies. They cried when they felt like it, ate when the urge hit and asked questions when the notion struck (sometimes at the most inopportune times) with no thought as to time or barrier.

Some of my fondest memories of my girls' childhood were the times they took up their rhythm band set and pranced around the house banging, pounding and clapping merrily. Sometimes during our family DATE WITH JESUS in the mornings, Chuck or I would play the piano and the girls would form a musical parade circling from the living room through the dining room and back to the living room. Their tiny faces beamed with joy and happy giggles sprang from their voices. What a delightful memory!

I often wonder what happens to us when we grow older. I suppose the cares of the world move in and crowd out the joy God intends for His little children to display. At the very moment we should be praising (in the midst of the cares), we choose to gripe. And I do believe griping is a choice just as happiness is a choice (see book by same name, Minirth & Meier). We choose everyday in any given situation the attitude we will reflect, whether one of thankfulness or one of irritableness.

I've been challenged in this department lately. Sometimes, (my family would probably say more than sometimes), I slide into a nasty, irritable mood that I can't seem to shake. When one practices irritability for as long as I have it becomes a hard and fast habit. Paul's words in

Chuck & Eileen Rife

Philippians 4:4 "Rejoice in the Lord always; again I will say rejoice" fall on deaf ears and are mumbled through clenched teeth. After all, the juicer's broken, the cat threw up, money is tight, the house is dirty and besides all that, I really don't feel well!

Amazing how much better I do feel when I relax in the midst of the cares and CHOOSE to praise instead of pout. Don't get me wrong. I don't think an attitude of praise and thankfulness necessarily means I'll fling out of bed in the morning with a pasted on smile, whirl into the kitchen and break dance on our shiny linoleum. (I've tried that, by the way. Doesn't seem to go over too well with the other sleepy members of the family). But I do believe God desires His people to operate out of quiet, peaceful hearts and an inner joy that comes from KNOWING God is in control. We CAN exhibit JOY in the midst of the mundane or in the midst of great pain if we are focused on the source of all JOY, the Lord Jesus Christ Himself!

That is what I shared that strange Sunday morning and I am challenged by my own words every day that I climb out of bed and breathe in the air of another day. I hope and pray that in some way you are also moved by them to the degree that you can be thankful for the life and marriage God has given you with all its variety, intrigue and wonder, and yes, at times, even boredom. Learn to tell the truth about your marriage, life and circumstances. The truth is God is in control and He is working all things according to His will. If you acknowledge this fact, you will see your life and your spouse in a different light — one which glows with praise and joyfulness!

PRACTICAL HELPS

Chuck & Eileen Rife
LEARNING TO BE THANKFUL IN YOUR MARRIAGE

PAUL'S FORMULA FOR SUCCESS AS FOUND IN PHILIPPIANS 4:4-13

TO DO: PAUL'S IMPERATIVES

1. Rejoice in your marriage (v.4).

2. Let your wife see your gentleness (v.5).

3. Pray together with thanksgiving (v.6).

4. Think correctly about one another and situations as they arise (v.8).

5. Act appropriately towards one another (v.9).

TO ENJOY: GOD AND ONE ANOTHER

1. God's contentment in your marriage (v.11)

2. God's power in your marriage (v.13)

3. God's peace in your marriage (vv.7, 9)

4. God's supply in your marriage (v.19)

Exercise:
✓ Read Philppians 4:4-9 aloud 5 times every morning and 5 times every evening for a week.

Marriage With An Attitude

✓ The following week add Philippians 4:10-13 to your readings. By the third week you will probably be able to quote the verses from memory.

Note: This is a great memory technique, but it is counterproductive to try to memorize the verses. Just enjoy the process as you hide God's Word in your heart.

GOOD THOUGHTS LIST-PHILIPPIANS 4:8

"Finally, brethren, whatever is true, whatever is honorable, whatever is right, whatever is pure, whatever is lovely, whatever is of good repute, if there is any excellence and if anything worthy of praise, let your mind dwell on these things."

✓ ***TRUE*** — being authentic and accurate
✓ ***HONORABLE*** — excellent, high moral character, honest
✓ ***RIGHT*** — correct principles, fair, righteous
✓ ***PURE*** — free from sin, guiltless, complete and true
✓ ***LOVELY*** — having a spiritual beauty, highly pleasing
✓ ***GOOD REPORT*** — a good description of a person or event
✓ ***EXCELLENCE*** — goodness, moral excellence and righteousness
✓ ***PRAISEWORTHY*** — deserving of approval or admiration

Using the above words, find examples from your marriage in the last twenty-four hours.

For Example:

TRUE: I am thankful that my wife told me the truth about the error she made in the checkbook.

Chuck & Eileen Rife

HONORABLE: I am thankful that my husband is faithful in our sexual relationship.

RIGHT: I am thankful that my wife is fair in dealing with the kids' issues.

PURE: I am thankful that my husband is pure in his actions towards me.

LOVELY: I am thankful that my wife is seeking God's ideals for her life.

GOOD REPORT: I am thankful that my husband is a good provider.

EXCELLENCE: I am thankful that my wife is faithful in her duties at home.

PRAISEWORTHY: I am thankful that my husband is sensitive to my needs.

Now it's your turn. Take the eight words from the list in Philippians 4:8 and write down examples from your marriage in the spaces provided. Repeat this exercise everyday for the next two weeks.

TRUE:

HONORABLE:

Marriage With An Attitude

RIGHT:

PURE:

LOVELY:

GOOD REPORT:

EXCELLENCE:

PRAISEWORTHY:

*I'm thinking about getting married.
I looked up the word 'engaged' in the dictionary.
It said, "To do battle with the enemy."
Then,
I looked up mother-in-law. It said, "See engaged!"*

Rachel A. Park

4
ATTITUDE OF SUPPLICATION
"Seeking the Source"
♥

"Dear Jesus, Can I have a DOLL tree like the one I saw at the bank this morning and that the pastor talked about in his sermon?" five-year-old Stephanie prayed while her mother listened on. Mom was bewildered trying to figure out what the pastor had preached on the previous Sunday. Finally, it dawned on her that his sermon had been on ADULTERY!

Michelle prayed, "Dear Jesus, please come and visit me at my house soon. I want to give this picture to You that I drew."

Rachel, wrestling with several profound issues of childhood, prayed, "Dear Jesus, do You hurt? Do You spank? Are You bigger than a rock? How does a bunny laugh? Lord, I know I'm not bigger yet, but I sure am growing up hard. Dear Jesus, please help Mom to be strong, so she can find my block."

Supplication is asking for what we want. Children find it so easy to do and in such a simple and straightforward manner that often we chuckle with amusement. A child's heart is open and receptive. In her mind, nothing is impossible. I suppose that is why Jesus said in the gospels that "unless a man become like a little child, he will not enter the kingdom of heaven" (Matthew 18:3).

Marriage With An Attitude

Children often sense the reality of God's presence in a greater way than adults and are convinced that God hears their prayers and will answer. We as adults should take a lesson or two from the little ones around us who seem to be tuned in to the Master's voice. Just like a child, we need to come before the Father with a ready faith that asks for the impossible and believes that God can accomplish incredible things on our behalf! Jesus modeled a life of prayer while on earth. Even as His disciples slept in the Garden of Gethsemane right before his fateful betrayal by Judas, Jesus petitioned the Father that this cup of sorrow and death might pass from Him. In the same breath He acknowledged God's sovereign will to do as His plan from ages past required — sending Jesus to the cross to redeem the world from sin. Once again, Jesus stepped down from His eternal throne, relinquished His right to free Himself and submitted Himself to God's plan of redemption. Jesus emptied Himself over and over again while on earth taking on the form of a bondservant because of the joy that lay on the other side of the cross. He asked, but God the Father said "NO, there is no other plan that can satisfy the righteous demands of My holiness. It breaks My heart, My Son, but You must go to the cross. There is no other way."

Many times we as believers, God's little children, come before His throne with our petitions. We ask, believing that in His mighty sovereignty He will work on our behalf according to His eternal will and plan for our lives. Sometimes, He says, "YES," other times "WAIT," and still other times, He gives us a flat-out "NO." Often, we do not understand. Especially hard are the No's that have no explanation. We wait and wait to see some sort of justification for His denial of the request, but no answer is found. Faith is tested and tried in the crucible of the unknown. Do we continue trusting a God who is silent? Do we keep asking for what He has clearly denied? Do we abandon our anxiety and simply lean on

Chuck & Eileen Rife

an all-wise heart who knows us better than ourselves and would never do anything to hurt His dear children? Hopefully, we will choose the latter, as we join in with the great preacher, Spurgeon, who once said, "God is too wise to be mistaken, and too good to be unkind."

One of Chuck's favorite verses since our courting days has been Psalm 37:4 which says, "Delight yourself in the Lord; and He will give you the desires of your heart." Early on in my Christian experience, I took the notion that anything I asked for, God was required to supply. Psalm 37:4 clearly specifies that it is only as I delight myself in the Lord that He will grant me my desires. **Delighting means placing God first in my life, over my spouse, my kids, my job, my hobby, TV, anything that would threaten that number one place that is reserved for Him alone. Delighting means spending time with Him each day, reading His words to me and talking to Him. Delighting means enjoying His presence and simply praising and worshipping Him for who He is.** The more I delight, the more He instills His godly desires within my heart, so that when I do make a request, more often than not, the supplication is in line with His will. My heart is living so close to His heart, that we now think alike. We want the same things.

So how does all this relate to asking for what we want within the context of marriage? I believe my first responsibility is to take a given request before the Lord. Sometimes, I will leave the item there and wait to see how God works it out. Other times, I will ask God for direction and then confront my spouse with the request. This is precisely where good communication skills are vital.

I Peter 3 lends some practical advice to each marriage partner in this area of asking our mates for what we want. While both partners are to practice submission towards

Marriage With An Attitude

one another the text clearly indicates that the wife's primary attitude toward her husband is to be one of submission. He is the head of the household, whether he is saved or unsaved. The saved wife may see her husband disobeying the Lord and request that he consider his relationship with God. Depending on the manner in which she approaches him with this delicate subject, he may choose to oblige her request or not. Since women tend to nag (sorry ladies; I know the truth hurts), I believe Peter included the winning your husband over "without a word" phrase, because often that technique is more effective than harping on an issue forever. I believe this applies to other confrontation issues as well, no matter how minor. Once the wife has expressed her viewpoint or request, either verbally or in writing, she should leave it alone. Continue to take the issue to the Lord and trust Him to work it out for the best. The husband carries ultimate responsibility for every family decision and will one day give an account before the Lord for how well he responded to this awesome duty.

Husbands are exhorted to "live with (their) wives in an understanding way, as with a weaker vessel, since she is a woman; and grant her honor as a fellow-heir of the grace of life, so that their (the husband's) prayers may not be hindered." (1 Peter 3: 7) One way to honor your wife is to listen to her requests and concerns. She is your equal, though functions within the home in a different capacity. She is a helper. Interestingly enough, God's response to your prayers seems to be in direct proportion to how well you honor your wife as an equal, listening to her concerns and input in the marriage.

As you both seek to honor one another through submission, openness and listening, you will often find that you share the same desires or at least are willing to compromise some of your own because you prefer the other person. You actually begin to regard your spouse as more important than yourself, not merely looking out for your own personal interests, but also for the interests of your mate (Philippians 2:3-4).

Sometimes a spouse will carry this idea of regarding the other as more important than himself to extremes. This is called codependency and takes on many varied forms. It is not our purpose here to look at this particular issue in-depth. Entire books have been written on this topic alone. However, we do feel that codependent problems greatly affect the balance and health of a marriage relationship and are worthy of consideration.

Oftentimes, a codependent spouse finds it quite difficult to ask for what they want. They are so consumed with meeting the needs of the other person that they are completely blinded to their own. A typical example of a codependent person is one who grew up in an alcoholic family. Learning early on to care for their abusive parent in order to keep peace or to survive, they denied their own feelings. After years of doing so, the denial pattern became fixed and surfaced itself in their marriage relationship. They learned to deaden their thoughts and feelings, to keep quiet and to doubt people. They developed a ravenous hunger for control because everything around them seemed out of control. They come to marriage with deep guilt, shame and fear of rejection, failure and abandonment. They do not know how to love themselves in order to effectively love other people, a strong Biblical principle.

A codependent spouse feels that they need to "fix" their mate. They operate out of an extreme lack of balance, attempting to rescue their spouse while personally risking drowning themselves. A codependent spouse is so out-of-balance that one person joked, "Before

Marriage With An Attitude

the codependent dies, someone else's life passes before his eyes."

Galatians 6:2 & 5 demonstrate the distinction between caring for others and caring for ourselves. Galatians 6:5 says, "For every man shall bear his own burden." In other words, God allows us a certain number of tasks and responsibilities each day to be accomplished with Christ's strength and for His glory. God wants us to read His Word, pray to Him, love our mates and families, work hard, fellowship with other believers and enjoy some rest and relaxation each day. Sound too ideal? Jesus says, "His yoke is easy and His burden is light." If we spend some time each day involved in the above pursuits, we remain strong and able to help our mates and others in balanced ways. We can truly do Galatians 6:2, which says, "Bear ye one another's burdens and so fulfill the law of Christ."

When someone allows his backpack to become an overburden, he needs extra help. The problem for a codependent is that they have a special built-in radar that seeks out burdened people. They can go to a party and their special radar takes them directly to the hurting, disillusioned and struggling people. Then they spend their whole evening offering unsolicited and often unappreciated help.

I counseled a mother who was dealing with excess stress in her life. I asked about the source of her stress and was curious when one of the things she mentioned was her agitation over the laundry at home. She explained that she was doing three loads of laundry a day because her seventeen year old son had gotten into the habit of taking three showers a day and using two big bath towels each time, immediately afterwards tossing them into the laundry basket. The dad in this picture was oblivious to the problem since his wife did not communicate with him

Chuck & Eileen Rife

concerning the issue and therefore was unaware that his son needed some change in his grooming habits.

She looked puzzled when I told her that today she got to graduate from doing her son's laundry. I directed her to go home, teach her son to do his laundry and never again do it for him. The next time I saw her she was glowing and reported that she did what I said and that her son actually learned to make one towel last the whole week!

Balance is the key word. When we balance our own backpack loads, then we are able to offer assistance to others. Part of the balancing process is being able to ask my spouse for what I need, without feelings of guilt or lack of control.

Think about piano movers. They always follow two very important principles. Have you ever helped move a piano? How many people were involved? More than just one, I bet. And yet that's the way we attempt to help others, all by ourselves. We need to let our mates and the Body of Christ do what they do best, work together in unity. Remember, one is a leg, another a hand, still another an arm, an eye, an ear and on the analogy goes. **No one person can do everything. We need each other.** Don't fall into the trap of, *you are the only one who understands. You are the only one I can trust. It's a set-up for developing your own piano-sized burden!*

So, the first principle of being an effective piano-mover is never go it alone. The second principle is limiting the burden time. Back to the moving illustration. When you moved your last piano how long did you have it hoisted up in the air? Not just rolling, pushing, or scooting the thing, but actually hoisting? Not long, hopefully, or you could have been seriously hurt. The same principle applies to helping people. To avoid

Marriage With An Attitude

burnout, limit the amount of time you spend helping other people.

Sometimes, we just need to learn to approach life a little differently. If you have been facing piano after piano with your mate you may need to begin to do things differently. In psychology class, I learned about the ***fourth cheeseless tunnel***. Scientists constructed a maze with four tunnels. At the end of the fourth tunnel they placed some cheese. Then they put rats into the maze. They immediately explored each tunnel since they could smell the cheese. As they proceeded through tunnel number one, to their disappointment, they found no cheese. They continued on into tunnel number two. They discovered no cheese. To prolong their agony, tunnel number three offered no cheese either. But when they rushed to tunnel number four, wah-lah, cheese at last!

The next day, the scientists conducted the same experiment. By the third day of experimentation, the rats stopped exploring tunnels one, two, and three. They went directly to tunnel number four and enjoyed their favorite cuisine. The next day, the scientists moved the cheese to tunnel number two. The rats immediately went to tunnel number four, but found no cheese. The lesson is quite simple. The difference between rats and humans is that the rats eventually began to explore other tunnels. Unfortunately, we humans tend to beat our heads against the wall saying, "I know that cheese was there" and refuse to explore other tunnels. We think things must always be the same.

As husbands, we believe that our wives should always respond the same way to our loving advances. After all, our logic teaches us that if our loving advances worked one day they ought to work every day, right? Wrong! Fourth cheeseless tunnel. Women are far too complex to reduce to a set of stimuli-response patterns. So, what are

Chuck & Eileen Rife

we men to do? Learn from the rats and begin to explore other tunnels. Uh! Change? Who, ME? No thanks! But that's the path towards oneness and intimacy with our mates. We need to encourage our wives to share their needs openly with us, so that we might minister to them more effectively. Learn from the rats; be courageous as a lion and gentle as a lamb. The reward will be true intimacy. Many patients I have worked with over the years are afraid to share their feelings with their spouses. How sad. They have had their feelings stepped on and invalidated.

One husband told his wife, "That's a stupid way to feel." In a situation like this, I begin the counseling process by helping both the husband and wife to understand how all feelings make sense, even if we do not like them. Our feelings are a product of our thoughts. Proverbs 23:7 teaches us that what we think will soon lead to corresponding feelings. It is okay to feel. God made us emotional as well as cognitive beings. When we understand how our thoughts and emotions are linked, we are better able to rejoice in the Lord, just as Paul did in Phil. 4:4 because we see life events and circumstances in the light of eternity, rather than just in reference to the particular moment. If I cannot talk to my spouse and I cannot share my deepest feelings with her, then I certainly cannot trust her. Trust is crucial in the marriage setting.

I remember a couple who came to me for counseling who did not trust each other at all. Before marriage, he had been a womanizer. Now he expected his wife to continually be unfaithful to him, so he scrutinized her every glance at men. He kept tabs on her so severely that he was constricting the life and joy right out of her. She never did trust him to provide since he had already been through multiple jobs and was currently on probation in his current job.

Marriage With An Attitude

Another lady once told me that her husband would constantly scoff at her ideas saying, "That's stupid! I'll tell you what to think!" Being devalued like that is devastating and cripples a relationship of mutual supplication.

A woman in her mid-fifties suffered severe sexual abuse in her teenage years. When she came to me for counseling, she was a picture of passive depression. She felt worthless and powerless. For years she blamed herself for what happened to her. When she learned to tell the truth about what happened to her she was then free to learn how to forgive. Her process of recovery ended in her sharing her story with others and encouraging them with Christ's love and forgiveness. Her face was different. Her demeanor and attitude were different. And, oh yes, her marriage was very different. Her husband thankfully declared, "I'm married to a new woman!"

If we are suffering with a codependent problem, the roots of guilt, shame and fear run very deep. Guilt is feeling bad for harmful things we DO. Shame is allowing the guilt to accumulate to such a point that we convince ourselves that this must be who we ARE. Then we negatively become self-fulfilling prophecies, continually living out the negative behavior that we are convinced is our lot. Only seeing ourselves through God's eyes can break this stranglehold of death. We learn to see ourselves as we are described in Ephesians 1:3-14. As Christians, Paul calls us chosen, holy, blameless, predestined, and redeemed. Wow! As we see ourselves through God's eyes, our lives are changed and our minds are transformed. As we lay all on the altar (Romans 12:1) and even put ourselves there, we are able to by faith trust God with our past. Then we are free to trust Him with our future and live in the present, knowing God is the one in control.

Chuck & Eileen Rife

Fear also runs deep for the codependent mate. They may be afraid of failure, rejection and abandonment. The fear of failure can keep them from asking for what they need. And it can keep them from trying new things, like writing this book, for example.

The fear of rejection can keep them at arm's length, holding their mate back, so they do not get too close. I counseled one couple who was having intimacy problems. It turned out that she was afraid to let him get too close to her for fear that he would discover her inner deficiencies and reject her.

Ultimately, the fear of abandonment dominates the marriage of a codependent spouse. God built us for relationships, first of all with Himself, then with our mates, with the Body of Christ at large and finally with outreach to the world with His gospel message. The worst fear known to man is not fear of snakes or even the fear of public speaking. It is the fear of being alone! This fear can drive a spouse to do too much for the other spouse, ignoring his own needs and desires and jeopardizing his own health and well being. Again, balance is the order for marital wholeness and being courageous enough to ask for what we need from one another in our marriages. Seek the source in supplication — God first and your spouse second.

I (Eileen) consider my parents, Bob and Lavina Hinkle, classic examples in this area of petition. They learned early on in their marriage how to petition God for their needs. They moved from New Jersey to Virginia to work with children through a faith mission organization called Children's Bible Mission (CBM). They were only there for a short time before moving to Tennessee to continue work with the mission. They have been there for over fifty years now. Well into their eighties, I have a

Marriage With An Attitude

deep respect for the dependence on God they have exhibited over the years. With very little money coming into the household and a handicapped son to care for, they relied heavily on God's resources, and He proved Himself time and time again on their behalf.

Not only did my parents learn to petition God, but they also learned how to petition one another for the things they each needed in the relationship. Their communication flows freely, but with the sensitivity to know when to drop an issue or not even bring it up for the moment. My dad particularly impresses me as a man who decided early that he did not need to have the last word in order to feel significant in their relationship. Time and time again I quietly watch him honor mom in this way. My mom impresses me as a woman who is cautious in sharing certain matters with dad and carefully thinks through important issues before bringing them up. To this day I still stand in awe of their love and devotion to one another after close to sixty years of marriage. They fit like a pair of well-worn shoes, all broken in and comfy.

In this area of supplication or asking for what we want, each spouse brings to the marital relationship differing expectations. The big four are money, sex, children and the in-laws. As we look more in-depth into the relationship, we can see many multi-faceted expectations in the areas of household management, yard work, entertainment options, roles, outside friendships and religious affiliations. It is crucial that good communication skills be employed in order to establish order and harmony in the home. Learning to ask for what you need or want and learning to appreciate and work with your spouse's needs is vital for a healthy, growing relationship.

Plan a time each day when you and your spouse can sit down together, uninterrupted and looking eyeball to

Chuck & Eileen Rife

eyeball, discuss your thoughts and concerns. Chuck and I personally find that mornings work best for us right after breakfast and family devotions. The devotions put us in a spirit of prayer and cooperation and prepare us for possible disagreement or confrontation. At first glance, this appears antithetical, when in reality, many times arriving at the discussion table means agreeing to disagree in a spirit of goodwill (No shouting matches, please). We each take a sheet of paper and for ten minutes we write on a designated topic or on individual concerns that we are currently facing. After ten minutes, we trade our papers, read them and either respond in writing or verbally. Each has a chance to air his viewpoint. Why do we choose writing as a primary mode of communication first? Because the writing process forces us to think through what we are going to say before the pen hits the paper. Often this does not happen when we speak first. We each try to state our case and focus on how we feel about a given issue. We endeavor to arrive at a joint solution or table the item until we have thought about it further. We have found that most concerns are minor and simply airing them gives rise to a logical solution. Because this area of communication is such a vital part of marriage we have included more practical helps at the end of this chapter. Practice the exercises with your spouse. As you learn what works best for you as a couple, you will come up with ideas of your own on how to communicate better. Remember, the content of communication is not the problem, the process is. Good communication takes hard work, but bad communication creates even more work! Communicating well is worth the effort!

Prayer is the most important tool you both have in learning to communicate well. Bring your concerns before the Father daily, both individually and as a couple. You will see a difference in how you relate together. Philippians 4:6,7 says, "Be anxious for nothing, but in

Marriage With An Attitude

everything by prayer and supplication with thanksgiving let your requests be made known to God. And the peace of God, which surpasses all comprehension, shall guard your hearts and your minds in Christ Jesus."

PRACTICAL HELPS

Marriage With An Attitude
HOW TO PETITION GOD

When communicating with your Heavenly Father, employ the **ACTS** *acrostic.*

A   ADORATION: Adore God for who He is in all His loveliness and divine attributes (Philippians 4:4).

C   CONFESSION: Confess or agree with God about any sin that may have broken fellowship with Him (1John 1:9).

T   THANKSGIVING: Thank God for His control in your circumstances, even though you may not understand the reasons behind them (Philippians 4:6).

S   SUPPLICATION: Bring your requests openly before your Father. Pray specifically (Philippians 4:6).

HOW TO PETITION YOUR SPOUSE

1. Pray before you begin.

2. If you feel like you might have trouble verbally expressing your request, write it down. Stick to one request at a time before moving to another.

3. Give your partner time to respond with his thoughts or ideas either verbally or in writing.

4. Compare thoughts on the request. Look for areas where you both agree.

5. You may need to agree to disagree on a particular request.

Chuck & Eileen Rife

For example, the wife may desire to remodel the living room, which will require a significant portion of the couple's savings. The husband is not as eager to tackle that particular project and would rather wait until they have saved more. He wishes to honor the wife's request, but just not now. They may choose to table the request until a later date. You can think of a request you may currently be dealing with and follow these guidelines. The key is respecting the other person's point of view and finding common ground from which to work.

6. Become a student of the other person. Ask information seeking what questions. Avoid judgmental why questions.

7. Any time the communication begins to get heated, go back to step 1.

We need to learn how to prefer one another, listen to one another and honor one another.

MARRIAGE EXPECTATION INVENTORY

Robert D. Kuest, D. Min. New Mission Systems, Int'l.
2565 E. Chapman Ave. Suite 211
Fullerton, CA 92831

Take a sheet of paper and answer the following questions as honestly as you can. Write down your own feelings about each topic, not your spouses.

Marriage With An Attitude

HOUSEHOLD EXPECTATIONS

What word comes to your mind when you consider this area? Duty, Joy, Wife's role, etc.

1. Type of living area you expect:

2. Division of chores, if any:

3. My idea of a clean house:

YARD EXPECTATIONS

What word comes to your mind when you consider this area?

1. Type of yard you desire:

2. Division of labor, if any, with grass, flower, vegetables, etc.:

ENTERTAINMENT EXPECTATIONS

What word comes to your mind when you consider this area?

1. TV or no TV? Viewing choices:

2. Dates out with your spouse: Where, When and How often:

3. Baby-sitter requirements:

4. Entertaining guests: When, How often:

5. Open to unannounced entertaining:

Chuck & Eileen Rife

MEAL EXPECTATIONS

What word comes to your mind here?

1. Division of labor, if any:

2. Number of meals, types, and times:

3. Snacks, if any:

SEXUAL EXPECTATIONS

What word comes to your mind in this area? Beautiful, Babies, Sinful, Dirty, Obligation, Love. Why?

1. Birth control, if any:

2. Responsibility for initiation of sex:

3. Amount (times a week, month, etc.):

CHILDREN

What comes to your mind in this area?

1. Amount:

2. Adoption option:

3. Natural childbirth:

4. Shared responsibilities in childcare:

5. Breastfeeding vs. bottle:

6. Time spent with various age children:

7. Sharing of discipline responsibilities:

8. To spank or not to spank:

9. Responsibility to answer questions concerning sex, life, relationships:

IN-LAWS

What word comes to your mind here?

1. Living arrangements (same town or out of town?)

2. Financial assistance from family:

3. Care of parents in old age:

4. Frequency of visits (to their home and to your home)

5. Number of phone calls:

FINANCIAL EXPECTATIONS

What do you think about when you consider your finances?

1. Feelings about your wife working:

2. Responsibility for the bills and check-writing:

3. Responsibility for insurance, annuities, retirement, etc.:

ROLE EXPECTATIONS

What do you think about when you consider this area?

1. Wife:

2. Husband:

COMMUNICATION EXPECTATIONS

What do you think about when you consider this area?

1. Frequency:

2. Setting or timing:

3. Your particular communication style (is it working? or do I need to change my style?):

RELIGIOUS EXPECTATIONS

What word comes to my mind when I think about this area?

1. Family devotions (times, places, whose responsibility?):

2. Involvement in church work (church choice, frequency, types, giving):

OUTSIDE FRIENDSHIPS

What do you think about when you consider this area of your relationship?

1. Mutual friends (how many, frequency of getting together):

2. Individual friends (how many, frequency of getting together):

CONCLUSION
Number from 1 to 10 the following in order of their importance in the marital relationship.

Marriage With An Attitude

_____Household responsibilities

_____Yard responsibilities

_____Social life

_____Meals prepared properly

_____Sexual relationship

_____Children

_____In-law relationships

_____Financial security

_____Communication

_____Religion

As you read the following sentences, select and circle the number that corresponds to the description that is most like your spouse.

1	2	3	4	5
Completely True	Partly True	Partly False / Partly True	Partly False	Completely False

1. My spouse talks with me about topics that are of interest to me.

   1   2   3   4   5

Chuck & Eileen Rife

2. My spouse allows me an adequate opportunity to talk about my feelings and activities.

1   2   3   4   5

3. My spouse is my best friend.

1   2   3   4   5

4. My spouse is aware of the times when I am feeling emotionally stressed.

1   2   3   4   5

5. My spouse readily gives compassion when I am suffering physically.

1   2   3   4   5

6. My spouse assumes some of my household and family responsibilities when I am not physically well.

1   2   3   4   5

7. My spouse frequently gives me unexpected gifts or does unexpected things for me.

1   2   3   4   5

8. My spouse and I go out alone at least once a month.

1   2   3   4   5

9. My spouse listens without judging when I share my fears.

1   2   3   4   5

Marriage With An Attitude

10. My spouse makes me feel that I am physically attractive to him/her.

1   2   3   4   5

11. My spouse makes me feel that I fill a need in his/her life that no one else can.

1   2   3   4   5

12. My spouse makes me feel that I am the only person with whom he/she desires physical intimacy.

1   2   3   4   5

(Source unknown)

PLAN OF ACTION SHEET

Areas I need to change in order to petition my spouse today:

Steps I need to take today to petition my spouse:

I'd like to go to an assertiveness training class. First, I need to check with my wife.

Rachel A. Park

EPILOGUE
ATTITUDE ACTS
CONCLUSION

In the movie, "*Cool Runnings*", John Candy reluctantly agrees to coach four young athletes with an impossible dream to become Jamaica's first Olympic bobsled team. The team makes it to Calgary to compete in a sport they know virtually nothing about, but with courage and determination to give it their all and the faith in one another to keep going, they live up to the challenge and soon become heroes.

Towards the end of the movie, Candy makes a penetrating statement to the driver of the bobsled team as he prepares for the final run the next day. Earlier, the young driver discovered that years before when Candy competed in the bobsled division, he cheated in order to win the gold, even though he had won the gold previously through skill alone. The serious Jamaican questions Candy, "Coach, why did you cheat? You had it all. I don't understand." Candy responded, "Well, you see, winning was my whole life and when winning is your whole life, you will do anything to win, but let me tell you something - a gold medal is a wonderful thing. But if you are not enough without it, you will never be enough with it." The driver questioned, "But Coach, how will I know if I am enough?" Candy responded, "When you cross that finish line, you'll know."

The purpose of this book has been to lead you to a deeper experience with God and as a result with your mate, to encourage you to adopt an attitude toward your spouse that Jesus has towards you. A mate that reflects humility, adoration, confession, thanksgiving and

Marriage With An Attitude

supplication towards God is one that will also reflect the same attitudes towards his spouse.

Foremost of all, God wants each of us to discover Him and to be enough with Him, not with anything or anyone else. So, if we have not learned to be enough with God alone, we will never be enough no matter who or what we accumulate. Building our marriages on the foundation of who God is and what He has accomplished on our behalf is absolutely essential to our peace and well-being on earth as well as our storing up treasures for eternity to come.

In her book, *God is in Control*, Twila Paris says, "Like every believer, I am called to love God above all else and to live a life of obedience to Him." If we are truly obedient to God's will, we will treat our mates in accordance with His Word — with respect, adoration, humility and thanksgiving in our hearts for one another.

Relationships are closer when we have that first and most important relationship with God. We love each other. We have conflict, because we are human and because we are alike in many ways and different in other ways. John 16:33 says, "In this world you will have tribulation..." and marriage is not exempt from this. Remember that your mate is not the enemy. Satan, the destroyer of relationships, is! Remember the love and common future that brought you together. Rehearse that positive memory often.

Learn to laugh at yourself. A good sense of humor can carry you over many a waterfall. Be honest about your limitations. Share your emotions positively. Men, don't be afraid to openly cry in front of your wife. She needs to see your tender heart. You will be a bigger man in her sight when you do. Don't take life too seriously; you won't get out alive anyway. Why waste time and energy over trivial concerns, many of which you have no control over to begin with. Take time out to be alone and nurture yourself. Knowing when you need some space and variation is healthy for a growing marriage. Date your spouse once a week. Our night is Friday and we try to preserve that time at all costs. We need that time to renew our love after a busy week and to focus on just each other for a couple of hours. Few things can compare to this investment in one another. And finally, in the words of Winston Churchill, "NEVER GIVE UP!" Success is inevitable because of PERSEVERANCE. Mistakes will happen, tempers will flare, failures will occur. Someone once commented, "It's not how many times you fall down, but how many times you get up that counts." Keep getting up in your marriage. You are worth it and so is your spouse.

Post this poem where you can read it often. It will be a reminder that you are not alone in your marital venture. It will be a constant reminder that with Christ as the head of your relationship you can develop a MARRIAGE WITH AN ATTITUDE—a Christlike attitude for HIS GLORY!

Marriage Takes Three

I once thought marriage took
Just two to make a go,
But now I am convinced
It takes the Lord also.

And not one marriage fails
Where Christ is asked to enter,
As lovers come together
With Jesus at the center.

But marriage seldom thrives
And homes are incomplete

Marriage With An Attitude

*Until He's welcomed there
To help avoid defeat.*

*In homes where Christ is first,
It's obvious to see,
Those unions really work,
For marriage still takes three.*

 —Perry Tanksley © used by permission

BIBLIOGRAPHY

William Hendriksen, *New Testament Commentary: Philippians,* Baker Book House Company, Grand Rapids, MI., 1962, p.100, 107-108.

Gary Smalley, *Hidden Keys to Loving Relationships;* Gary Smalley Relationship Center, 1987, 1-800-848-6329, www.garysmalley.com

John Powell, *Why Am I Afraid to Tell You Who I Am?* Argus Communications, 1969.

Ed Wheat, *Love Life For Every Married Couple,* Zondervan Publishing House, 1980, 1987, brief synopsis of chapter 13. Used by permission.

Philip J. Myers, *Family Seminar Syllabus,* Miami Christian College, Appendix G.

Gary Chapman, *The Five Love Languages,* Moody Press, Chicago, 1992. Used by permission.

Rachel A. Park, *Comedy Comes Clean,* e-mail-juno.com.

Billy and Janice Hughey, *A Rainbow of Hope,* Rainbow Studies, Inc., El Reno, Oklahoma, 1994, p.188.

Marriage With An Attitude

Hannah Smith, *The Christian's Secret of a Happy Life,* Old Tappan, N.J.: Revell, 1942, pp.153-154.

Twila Paris, *God Is in Control,* Warner Press, Mexico, 1994.

Perry Tanksley, Dear Cards, P.O. Box 1197, Clinton, MS.

Chuck & Eileen Rife
FOUNDATIONS FOR SUCCESSFUL FAMILIES

Reading and Resource List compiled by:
Total Life Counseling
5372 Fallowater Lane, Suite A
Roanoke, Virginia 24014
(540) 989-1383
Fax (540) 989-8092

Bustanoby, Andre; *Just Talk To Me:Talking and Listening For a Happier Marriage* — Zondervan-1971

Carter, Les; *Prodigal Spouse* — Nelson-1990

Chapman, Gary ; *The Five Love Languages* — Northfield-1992

Cloud, Henry & Townsend, John; *Boundaries* — Zondervan-1992

Crabb, Larry; *Inside Out* — Navpress-1988
Men and Women: Enjoying the Differences — Zondervan-199
The Marriage Builder — Pyranee-1982

Dobson, James; *Love Must Be Tough* — Word-1983
What Wives Wish Husbands Knew About Divorce — Tyndale-1975
Straight Talk to Men and Their Wives — Word-1980

Farrel, Bill & Pam and Conway, Jim & Sally; *Pure Pleasure: Making Your Marriage a Great Affair* — Intervarsity-1994

Getz, Gene; *The Measure of a Family* — Regal-1976

Gray, John; *Men are from Mars, Women are from Venus* — Harper-Collins-1992

Hansel, Tim; Through *the Wilderness of Loneliness* — Life Journey Books-1991
Holy Sweat — Word-1987
When I Relax, I feel Guilty — LifeJourney Books-1979

Marriage With An Attitude

Harley, Willard; *His Needs, Her Needs* — Revell-1986

Landorf, Joyce; *I Came to Love You Late* — Revell-1977

Luecke, David; *The Relationship Manual for Couples: How to Diagnose, Build, Or Enrich a Relationship* — The Relationship Institute 1981

Mains, Karen Burton; *You are What You Say* — Zondervan-1988

Minirth, Frank & Mary Alice, et al. *Passages of Marriage* — Nelson-1991

Patterson, Ben; *Waiting* — Intervarsity Press-1989

Penner, Clifford & Joyce; *A Gift for All Ages* A Family Handbook on Sexuality — Word-1986

The Gift of Sex: A Christian Guide to Sexual Fulfillment — Word-1981

Rainey, Dennis & Barbara; *Staying Close* — Ward-1989
The Questions Book for Marriage Intimacy — FamilyLife-1988

Smalley, Gary; *If He Only For Better or For Best Hidden Keys to Loving Relationships Knew* (Videotape) Zondervan- — Zondervan-1979
Relationships Today - 1991

Smalley, Gary w/ Janssen, Al; *Joy That Lasts* — Zondervan -1986

Smalley, Gary & Trent, John; *The Language of Love* — Focus on the Family 1988

Sneed, Sharon & Joe McIlhaney; *PMS* — Baker-1988

Stott, John; The Message of the *Sermon on the Mount* (Matthew 5-7) — The Intervarsity Press-1978

Warren, Neil Clark; *The Triumphant Marriage* — Focus on the Family-1995

Wheat, Ed; *Love Life* — Zondervan -1980

Wheat, Ed & Gaye; *Intended for Pleasure* — Revell- 1977

Williams, H.Page; *Do Yourself A Favor: Love Your Wife* — Bridge -1973

Wright, H. Norman; *Communication: Key to Your Marriage* — Regal -1974

Chuck & Eileen Rife

Yates, John & Susan; *What Really Matters At Home*   Word -1992

Chuck & Eileen Rife

HOW TO RECEIVE CHRIST AS YOUR PERSONAL SAVIOUR

1. Admit that you are a sinner (Romans 3:23) "For all have sinned and come short of the glory of God." *(Romans 6:23)* "For the wages of sin is death, but the free gift of God is eternal life in Jesus Christ our Lord."

2. Believe that Jesus died on the cross in your behalf and rose again from the grave (Romans 5:8) "But God demonstrates His own love toward us, in that while we were yet sinners, Christ died for us."

3. Receive Jesus into your life for the forgiveness of your sin (Romans 10:9,10,13) "that if you confess with your mouth Jesus as Lord and believe in your heart that God raised Him from the dead, you shall be saved; for with the heart man believes, resulting in righteousness, and with the mouth he confesses, resulting in salvation. FOR WHOEVER WILL CALL UPON THE NAME OF THE LORD WILL BE SAVED."

You can pray this prayer right now if you desire to receive Jesus:

Lord, I confess that I am a sinner. I cannot save myself. I believe that You sent Your Son, Jesus, into the world to die on the cross for my sin and to rise again from the grave to be my living Saviour. I do receive You now. Come into my life, forgive my sins and change me with Your power. Thank-you for hearing my prayer and saving me.
Amen.

Marriage With An Attitude

If you received Jesus as your Saviour just now, we would love to hear from you. Write us at:

Chuck/Eileen Rife
5534 Cove Rd.
Roanoke, Va. 24019
or by e-mail at: marriage3@juno.com.

Take positive steps to read your Bible daily and talk to God. Get into a good Bible-believing church that preaches the Word of God. Tell someone else about your newfound faith. These are ways you will grow in your knowledge of God.

GOD BLESS YOU!

Chuck & Eileen Rife

MARRIAGE WITH AN ATTITUDE

BOOK AND SEMINAR INFORMATION
1 (540) 562-1632 or marriage3@juno.com

To order additional copies of:
 MARRIAGE WITH AN ATTITUDE
Complete the information below.

Ship to: (Please print)

Name_____

Address_____

City_____ State_____
Zip_____

Day phone_____

_____copies of *MARRIAGE WITH AN ATTITUDE*

 $10.00 per book $_____

Postage and handling @ $3.00 PER BOOK $_____
Virginia residents add   4.5% sales tax $_____

Total amount enclosed $_____

Make checks payable to **Chuck or Eileen Rife**

Send to: Chuck/Eileen Rife
5534 Cove Rd.
Roanoke, Virginia 24019

Marriage With An Attitude

To schedule a seminar in your area, please contact Chuck/Eileen Rife at 5534 Cove Rd. Roanoke, Virginia, 24019 or by e-mail: marriage3@juno.com.

Our four-hour marriage seminar is based on our book, *MARRIAGE With An Attitude,* and incorporates lecture, discussion, humor, music and drama.

Flyers are available upon request.